Mexican American Women, Dress, and Gender

Mexican American women have endured several layers of discrimination deriving from a strong patriarchal tradition and a difficult socioeconomic and cultural situation within the US ethnic and class organization. However, there have been groups of women who have defied their fates at different times and in diverse forms.

Mexican American Women, Dress, and Gender observes how *Pachucas*, *Chicanas*, and *Cholas* have used their body image (dress, hairstyle, and body language) as a political tool of deviation; and intends to measure the degree of intentionality in said oppositional stance. For this purpose and, claiming the sociological power of photographs as a representation of precise sociohistorical moments, this work analyzes several photographs of women of said groups with the aim of proving the relevance of "other" body images in expressing gender and ethnic identification, or disidentification from the mainstream norm.

Proposing a diachronic, comparative approach to young Mexican American women, this monograph will appeal to students and researchers interested in Chicano History, Race and Ethnic Studies, American History, Feminism, and Gender Studies.

Amaia Ibarraran-Bigalondo is a lecturer at the University of the Basque Country, Spain.

Routledge Research in Gender and Society

Masculinities, Sexualities and Love
Aliraza Javaid

Body, Migration, Re/constructive Surgeries
Making the Gendered Body in a Globalized World
Edited by Gabriele Griffin and Malin Jordal

Gender and Migration
Intersectional Prospects
Anna Amelina and Helma Lutz

Gender and Precarious Research Careers
A Comparative Analysis
Edited by Annalisa Murgia and Barbara Poggio

Prostitution, Pornography and Trafficking in Women
Israel's Blood Money
Esther Hertzog and Erella Shadmi

Mexican American Women, Dress, and Gender
Pachucas, Chicanas, Cholas
Amaia Ibarraran-Bigalondo

Trauma, Women's Mental Health, and Social Justice
Pitfalls and Possibilities
Emma Tseris

Wellness in Whiteness
Biomedicalisation and the Promotion of Whiteness and Youth among Women
Amina Mire

For more information about this series, please visit: www.routledge.com/sociology/series/SE0271

Mexican American Women, Dress, and Gender

Pachucas, Chicanas, Cholas

Amaia Ibarraran-Bigalondo

LONDON AND NEW YORK

First published 2019
by Routledge
2 Park Square, Milton Park, Abingdon, Oxon OX14 4RN

and by Routledge
52 Vanderbilt Avenue, New York, NY 10017

First issued in paperback 2020

Routledge is an imprint of the Taylor & Francis Group, an informa business

© 2019 Amaia Ibarraran-Bigalondo

The right of Amaia Ibarraran-Bigalondo to be identified as author of this work has been asserted by her in accordance with sections 77 and 78 of the Copyright, Designs and Patents Act 1988.

All rights reserved. No part of this book may be reprinted or reproduced or utilised in any form or by any electronic, mechanical, or other means, now known or hereafter invented, including photocopying and recording, or in any information storage or retrieval system, without permission in writing from the publishers.

Trademark notice: Product or corporate names may be trademarks or registered trademarks, and are used only for identification and explanation without intent to infringe.

British Library Cataloguing-in-Publication Data
A catalogue record for this book is available from the British Library

Library of Congress Cataloging-in-Publication Data
A catalog record for this book has been requested

ISBN 13: 978-0-367-67156-3 (pbk)
ISBN 13: 978-0-367-10942-4 (hbk)

Typeset in Times New Roman
by Apex CoVantage, LLC

To My Magnificent Eight
They Know

Contents

Acknowledgments ix
A note to the reader x

Introduction 1

1 **Dress, clothing, fashion, and style** 8
   1.1. The function of dress 10
   1.2. Clothing, fashion, and style 12

2 **The 20th century and fashion** 20

3 **Style, subcultures, and Mexican American women** 25

4 ***Pachucas*: breaking the norm in the Forties** 33
   4.1. Life and expectations for US women in the Forties 33
      4.1.1. World War II and Mexican American women 35
   4.2. Women's fashion in the Forties 37
   4.3. The Pachuca: *a rebel without a cause 39*
      4.3.1. Pachucas, Pachucos, and the Zoot Suit Riots 39
      4.3.2. The Pachuca *style politics 44*

5 ***Chicanas*: fighting the norm in the Seventies** 55
   5.1. Life and expectations for US women in the Seventies 55
   5.2. Women's fashion in the Sixties 59
   5.3. El Movimiento Chicano and la Chicana *60*
   5.4. The Chicana *style politics 65*
      5.4.1. The Brown Berets 67
      5.4.2. The Chicana *feminist activists 74*

6 *Cholas*: adapting to other norms in the Nineties   87
   6.1. Life and expectations for US young women in the Nineties 87
   6.2. Women's fashion in the Nineties 89
   6.3. Gangs and Cholo/a *style in 20th century* barrios *91*
      6.3.1. The girls in/around the gang system: Cholas *93*
   6.4. The Chola *style politics 96*

7 Concluding remarks   105

Bibliography   109
Index   115

Acknowledgments

This work arose as a mixture of an academic and a personal drive. An academic one, because that is what I am now. A personal one, because the need to connect the personal to the academic has always been there, in me. This is, thus, a personal work, which could never have been accomplished without the help and support of many. First, without the love and support of my family, of Malen and Nora, who have always enjoyed coming to the other side of the world with me, where ama goes to University every morning. Of Diego, who has always understood me, and supported me unconditionally, in his way. Of Felipe and Karmele, my parents, who have made an effort as big as mine throughout all these years, understanding and respecting my difference during my young, loco years, and today, accompanying me to the other side of the world, physically, him, and emotionally and spiritually, her. Of Irantzu and Awa, who are always with me, here and there, in our side of the world, and in the other, too. Of Josu, for being who he is. Difference makes you the best, my dearest bro. I love you all dearly. Of María Herrera-Sobek, a source of inspiration, academic and personal. I owe you a lot, María. Of Francisco Lomelí, who has always been ready to help and welcome me. Thank you both, very sincerely. Of my beloved friends, Esti and Yolanda, I could not live without our daily conversations and confessions, you are the best friends and colleagues one could ever have. Of all my friends at the UPV/EHU (David, thank you for taking me out for coffee, always), and those outside University. I am who I am thanks to you, too. Of the happiest, most energetic person and friend, Virginia. You saved this project. It will happen next time. Of all those friends who were happy to know it was happening. You are all important to me. Of all those who wanted but could not help, Beni, David, Senen. What great artists you are. Of all the institutions that supported me in this way: USAC, MINECO (project code: FFI2014–52738-P), of the REWEST team (Grupo Consolidado IT1206–16) (thank you Angel for following me; thanks, David, for making this up). Of those who, without knowing me, tried to help: special thanks to Catherine Ramírez, Simon Elliot, Diego Vigil, Devra Weber, Luis C. Garza, and many others. I wish there were more people like you. And why not, of those who did not want to help.

Thank you all. Next time it will all be different.

A note to the reader

I started writing this book out of curiosity and as a personal drive. My career as an academic started as long as 20 years ago. Or maybe more. Maybe my career as an academic started when I first took an American Literature class with my much-admired lecturer then, and friend and colleague later, Vickie Olsen. I was young and looked 'different' then. And I knew it, and I liked it and I probably consciously looked for it. It was the end of the Eighties and the Basque Country, where I was born and raised, was a sociologically, culturally and politically intense place. Too intense, probably, but that was what it was. In that intense sociocultural and political situation, young people rebelled. Some became fiercely nationalistic, others complied to the norm and some (including myself) were fascinated by a powerful alternative, pseudo-anarchist movement, where angry punk music, occupied and self-managed cultural spaces (*Gaztetxes* – young people's homes, in Basque) seemed a useful and creative way out from an aggressive Basque nationalism and an harsh state machine. But I was always 'in between': rebellious and alternative as I looked, I never left what was considered 'the right path' in the Nineties. And in an unplanned and probably too-easy way, I became an active part of academia. I got a job at the University of the Basque Country after I obtained my Ph.D. degree with a doctoral thesis on Feminist Chicana Literature. Everything was fascinating to me. I was fascinated by those emerging voices who were different, who described and praised difference and yet were constructive and (r)evolutionary. But even within academia, I felt different, and I liked being different. I probably wanted to be different. And, once inside, I very much wanted to contribute to the creation of a different academic world, where lecturers and academics looked at 'the real world,' with its 'real issues.' Teaching literature seemed a great way to produce some impact, to provoke a little change, at least in those who read with me.

Years have passed and I still feel I do not totally fit. I still believe the gap between the theoretical world and the practical one does not need to be an untrespassable border. And I still believe in change, revolutions and . . . why not . . . in the power of youth as a catalyst of change. I am very probably very much part of the system, but I still feel an attraction for difference, youth expression and the power of diversity. And for subcultures, and for women within subcultures. And for the claim of a female voice and agency within subcultures.

This is why the following work is not a purely academic work. It is a subjective personal vision of somebody who once looked different and wanted to express change, and disconformity (why not), but also creativity and the hope for a better future, as well as individual (female) agency through her attire, through her group affiliation, and in sum, through her body. Her body and looks as lived experience, as a "concrete lived entity" (De Clerq 4). It is the subjective personal vision of a once 'street girl' who has read widely about the way other 'street girls' (*Chicanas, Pachucas* and *Cholas*) have been represented. It is the subjective personal view of an academic who wanted to look at the way other 'street girls' represent and present their bodies and selves as "concrete and lived" bodies.

In sum, this is not a book that intends to draw any feminist theoretical conclusion(s), nor does it start from any concrete theoretical background or wants to adhere its findings to any theoretical trend. This is not a deep ethnographic or sociological research work that aims to reach categorizing or labeling conclusions on any issue regarding 'the *Pachuca/Chicana/Chola* experience.' This book is not based on the compilation of scientific data, but on a few representations of different women (whom I deeply respect), found openly and freely in diverse sources, which have helped me identify myself with the represented ones and thus draw some observations on the signification of their representations.

This book is, in sum, the result of my still (I think) revolutionary spirit, of my deep belief that women and girls still need to be different and break rules, that the fight is not over and that difference is political. Because, borrowing Angharad Valdivia and Rhiannon Bettivia's words, "the intellectual is the personal is the political" (24). Because lived lives are political and one's position in life, towards life and towards oneself and others is always political. And needs to seek for change and (r)evolution.

Introduction

> An image is worth a thousand words.

Personal image is a mark of personal identity. Gender is a mark of personal identity. According to this simple, yet intricate formula, personal image and gender are related. Gender, already proved as a social construction, undoubtedly marks the social identity of an individual. Women, or women who "become women" (De Beauvoir 330) through the influx of the society they live in and its regulating norms and cultural values, are thus expected to adopt a particular attitude, demeanor and image, which directly links them to the category of women as individuals and as a homogeneous group. And so are men. The roles of men and women throughout the different periods and spans of time of Western civilization have varied and adapted to the times. In all cases, these have always been conditioned by diverse nonpersonal, but social and cultural norms. Among these, the influence of religion (Christianity, in particular) as a set system of beliefs and social and moral conduct has clearly established said roles and particularly those of women, whose lives, destinies and even ways of acting, behaving and showing themselves in public have been clearly defined by such religious practices and beliefs. Morality, decency and the overall ethical position of women have, in most cases, been imposed upon them by said set of social and cultural norms of conduct. Among these, the way a woman should look has been of uttermost relevance to measure her adaptability or disconformity to the norm, and thus her morals and respectability.

In this context, and leaving aside the particular cultural and social norms related to womanhood, femininity and female behavior, women, since time immemorial, have been required to dress and act 'as women' and in a 'womanly fashion.' The first written words on female appearance are found in the Bible, where dress is portrayed as a punishment for the loss of paradise and the revelation of a world marked by sin and salvation/condemnation.

> When the woman saw that the tree produced good food, was attractive in appearance, and was desirable for making one wise, she took some of its fruit

norms with their clothes and 'irreverent' behavior, which, like their male peers, was considered a betrayal of the community. The *Pachuco* male's zoot suit, his use of an 'altered' version of English and a similarly 'altered' version of Spanish, *Caló*, his defiant style and forms and, in sum, his inconformity and displacement, made him the symbol of the first subversive and anti-system individual within the Mexican American community, whose cultural heritage is alive today. In fact, his language style, which marked his difference, "was an inventive, living language, and thus hard to pin down, but certain key features and typical terms can be detailed. Historically, the name *Caló* itself refers to *zincalo*, the language of the Gypsies in 15th century Spain, who brought to Mexico many words" (Macías 87). Nowadays, *Caló*, despite its underground origins, represents "a bona fide linguistic variety of Southwest Spanish spoken by *Chicanos* and *Chicanas* from various social and economic backgrounds" (Macías 89).

The *Pachuca*, moreover, crossed the boundaries and limits marked by the religious and moral standards of the community, and her 'provocative' dress, hairstyle and makeup soon brought her to the condition of *Malinche*, or betrayer of the group. *Pachucas* were considered loose and frivolous women both within and outside the group. Theirs, however, was a big step towards the acquisition of a female agency, which would decades later be articulated in the form of what would be called '*Chicana* feminism.' Lacking an elaborate intellectual feminist discourse, their style and attitude became subversive *per se*.

The ensuing decades, the Sixties and Seventies, were times of activism and consciousness gaining for many groups and collectives. *Chicanos* were no different, and they organized themselves into an articulated movement, the *Movimiento Chicano*, which called for the demand of equal rights for the group, and their full acceptance within the mainstream social arrangement, together with the defense of their cultural heritage and difference. The *Chicana* feminists, who not only struggled for the recognition of the Mexican American community, but also for the claim of their specificity as women, soon saw themselves needing to stand out both from their men and the mainstream feminists, as the former did not recognize their upgraded discrimination as women and the latter their added difficulties due to their class and ethnic particularities. *Chicana* feminism, therefore, was a conscious movement, which not only occurred 'in the streets,' but was accompanied by an elaborate system of ideas, philosophical and theoretical writings, literature, art, etc. In this context, most of the women who adhered to the *Chicana* movement were women with a strong political consciousness who expressed their oppositional stance not only on conceptual grounds, but also in practical terms.

Lastly, *Cholas*, or young *barrio* girls, who are often associated in terms of their physical appearance with the gang subculture, also identify as part of this group through their style and dress code. Dwellers of some of the most underprivileged areas of their cities, these young women experience the difficulties associated with a lack of educational and personal opportunities. In this context, some of these girls find in the gang system a safe haven that provides them with a 'life chance.' In it, some of the most constraining gender roles are clearly reproduced.

Introduction

> An image is worth a thousand words.

Personal image is a mark of personal identity. Gender is a mark of personal identity. According to this simple, yet intricate formula, personal image and gender are related. Gender, already proved as a social construction, undoubtedly marks the social identity of an individual. Women, or women who "become women" (De Beauvoir 330) through the influx of the society they live in and its regulating norms and cultural values, are thus expected to adopt a particular attitude, demeanor and image, which directly links them to the category of women as individuals and as a homogeneous group. And so are men. The roles of men and women throughout the different periods and spans of time of Western civilization have varied and adapted to the times. In all cases, these have always been conditioned by diverse nonpersonal, but social and cultural norms. Among these, the influence of religion (Christianity, in particular) as a set system of beliefs and social and moral conduct has clearly established said roles and particularly those of women, whose lives, destinies and even ways of acting, behaving and showing themselves in public have been clearly defined by such religious practices and beliefs. Morality, decency and the overall ethical position of women have, in most cases, been imposed upon them by said set of social and cultural norms of conduct. Among these, the way a woman should look has been of uttermost relevance to measure her adaptability or disconformity to the norm, and thus her morals and respectability.

In this context, and leaving aside the particular cultural and social norms related to womanhood, femininity and female behavior, women, since time immemorial, have been required to dress and act 'as women' and in a 'womanly fashion.' The first written words on female appearance are found in the Bible, where dress is portrayed as a punishment for the loss of paradise and the revelation of a world marked by sin and salvation/condemnation.

> When the woman saw that the tree produced good food, was attractive in appearance, and was desirable for making one wise, she took some of its fruit

> and ate it. Then she also gave some to her husband who was with her, and he ate some, too. As a result, they both understood what they had done, and they became aware that they were naked. So they sewed fig leaves together and made loincloths for themselves.
>
> (Genesis 3: 6–7)

Ever since the first 'act of dressing,' clothing and the choice (or imposition) of a certain kind of clothing has been provided with meaning and social indication. Class division, gender separation, age, geographical origin, education and/or spousal status are just a few of the social indicators that have been conveyed by dress and clothes since the beginning of 'dressed' times. The external appearance of an individual, of a woman in this particular case, positions her in a certain social and cultural category, and hence clothes and other nonverbal physical markers are and have been essential for the configuration of a stratified social arrangement where some are on the top and many on the bottom lines. This work, however, is not aimed at understanding and analyzing the construction of dress and clothing as a social marker, but, on the contrary, the means by which dress and clothing (and other nonverbal physical markers) subvert said stratified sociocultural arrangement and create new methods of personal and group identification and visualization.

In the contemporary world, where the abundance of images is marking the modern-day construction of cultural meaning and norms, the relevance of the personal external image is indubitable. Television, the publishing industry, cinema and fashion, among others, have become the creators and perpetuators of the standards of beauty, gender identity, social status and even ideological affiliation. In the case of Western societies, women have been required to follow and respect a strict dress code, which positions them at a certain status and connects them to others of their same condition. Thus, women in the upper classes dressed to dwell among the upper classes and lower-class women were also required to follow the norms and standards of the beauty and dress code. In sum, clothing performs a specific function: clothes cover nudity, they safeguard the intimacy of individuals, protect them from natural forces and, in another sphere, clothing conveys social and cultural meaning. In this context, following the dress code of a particular time and period implies accepting the sociocultural norms of the times, whereas subverting it and breaking the boundary established by this code becomes a (sub)conscious revolutionary act.

In the case of young people in the 20th century, the conscious adherence to the social norm or its subversion has been performed, among other means, through the assimilation or rejection of a set of physical traits and looks often represented by clothing choices. Considering the fact that "a fashion is any style that has gained widespread acceptance in a given period" (Horn 13) and that "it is dependent upon the willingness of the majority to conform to it" (Horn 14), one's clothing choices position the individual on one side or another of the social norm. In the case of the young collectives that defy such a norm and are thus considered subcultural, group identification and affiliation is, among other means, achieved by the communal adoption of a particular divergent dress and style in general (which includes clothing, hairstyle, language, body gestures, musical taste, etc.).

In the particular case of Mexican American women, the protagonists of this work, the dress and behavioral code conceived for women has been intricately related to the Christian religious and moral tradition of the group. Religious and cultural icons such as *La Virgen de Guadalupe* or *La Llorona* have established and perpetuated the image of the Mexican American woman as a silent, enduring woman, respectful and proud of the cultural heritage of her group, and thus bearer and continuator of the tradition. The relevance of the figure of the mother as the only role possible for women has maintained the idea of the Mexican American family as the nucleus of the internal arrangement of the community. Within this, gender roles are clearly marked and accepted, and women fulfill that of being the domestic, private figure who preserves the continuation of the communal values. This role, moreover, not only implies a certain number of principles such as the ones mentioned before, but also marks clear attitudinal requirements, where dress code and physical appearance are included. Mexican American women, particularly in the case of the women focus of this study, all of them living in different periods of the 20th century, were not meant to 'stand out' or be noteworthy, but they should keep to themselves and their peers. The static image of the *Virgen de Guadalupe* best exemplifies the way a 'woman should be,' a good, discreet, calm woman, whose physicality had to be hidden inside her clothes.

As previously stated, clothing, as a conveyor of a system of meaning and significance, can not only suggest acceptance of the norm and status quo, but can clearly imply a direct opposition to said equilibrium. Regardless of the fact that the vast majority of women of Mexican American origin of the 20th century accepted said norms and rules, the focus of this work is aimed at those who dared defy the norms and speak for themselves. In particular, this work will look at the women who made use of diverse tools to be seen and heard. This will be observed through their clothing choices, look and attitude sometimes, or through elaborated political agendas and discourses in other cases. As an example, *Pachucas*, young girls who became the target of the group's suspicion and disregard during the decade of the Forties, dared subvert the code of gender roles established within the community. In a social context marked by World War II, North American women (and Mexican Americans too) were allowed to enter the workforce in the expanding arms manufacturing industry. This chance provided women with an economic freedom they had lacked until now, turning them into potential targets of the expanding consumerism. In the same manner, this economic capability brought women into public spaces, as they accessed the leisure world, which occurred 'out in the streets.' Fashion and clothing also marked the newly acquired female agency, and women became likewise the targets of the beauty industry. Mexican American women, similarly, entered the workforce, in a symbolically radical step that represented the 'abandonment' of the family home, the traditional, community-centered domestic space. *Pachucas*, to be specific, broke all norms with their clothes and 'irreverent' behavior, which, like their male peers, was considered a betrayal of the community. The *Pachuco* male's zoot suit, his use of an 'altered' version of English and a similarly 'altered' version of Spanish, *Caló*, his defiant style and forms and, in sum, his inconformity and displacement, made him the symbol of the first subversive and anti-system individual within the Mexican American community, whose cultural heritage is alive today. In fact, his language style, which marked his difference, "was an inventive, living language, and thus hard to pin down, but certain key features and typical terms can be detailed. Historically, the name *Caló* itself refers to *zincalo*, the language of the Gypsies in 15th century Spain, who brought to Mexico many words" (Macías 87). Nowadays, *Caló*, despite its underground origins, represents "a bona fide linguistic variety of Southwest Spanish spoken by *Chicanos* and *Chicanas* from various social and economic backgrounds" (Macías 89).

The *Pachuca*, moreover, crossed the boundaries and limits marked by the religious and moral standards of the community, and her 'provocative' dress, hairstyle and makeup soon brought her to the condition of *Malinche*, or betrayer of the group. *Pachucas* were considered loose and frivolous women both within and outside the group. Theirs, however, was a big step towards the acquisition of a female agency, which would decades later be articulated in the form of what would be called '*Chicana* feminism.' Lacking an elaborate intellectual feminist discourse, their style and attitude became subversive *per se*.

The ensuing decades, the Sixties and Seventies, were times of activism and consciousness gaining for many groups and collectives. *Chicanos* were no different, and they organized themselves into an articulated movement, the *Movimiento Chicano*, which called for the demand of equal rights for the group, and their full acceptance within the mainstream social arrangement, together with the defense of their cultural heritage and difference. The *Chicana* feminists, who not only struggled for the recognition of the Mexican American community, but also for the claim of their specificity as women, soon saw themselves needing to stand out both from their men and the mainstream feminists, as the former did not recognize their upgraded discrimination as women and the latter their added difficulties due to their class and ethnic particularities. *Chicana* feminism, therefore, was a conscious movement, which not only occurred 'in the streets,' but was accompanied by an elaborate system of ideas, philosophical and theoretical writings, literature, art, etc. In this context, most of the women who adhered to the *Chicana* movement were women with a strong political consciousness who expressed their oppositional stance not only on conceptual grounds, but also in practical terms.

Lastly, *Cholas*, or young *barrio* girls, who are often associated in terms of their physical appearance with the gang subculture, also identify as part of this group through their style and dress code. Dwellers of some of the most underprivileged areas of their cities, these young women experience the difficulties associated with a lack of educational and personal opportunities. In this context, some of these girls find in the gang system a safe haven that provides them with a 'life chance.' In it, some of the most constraining gender roles are clearly reproduced.

The boys become the providers and the girls their companions and mothers of their offspring. In fact, the statistics prove that the rates of teen pregnancy among young *barrio* girls are high. According to the National Centers for Disease Control and Prevention's data, even if the numbers have almost been halved during the last 20 years, Hispanic teenagers show the highest rates of pregnancies (as of the year 2013).[1] The gang, as a highly hierarchized and organized group, clearly establishes the roles of its members, as well as their codes of behavior. Among these, the style politics performed by the groups (characterized by a particular dress code, tattoos and body language) are a mark of belonging, and define them as members of a particular *clicka* (gang). Women in the gangs (or who exist around the gangs), as part of this system, reproduce the dress codes established by the group, and as such identify with the rest through their style and body politics. Interestingly, this dress code makes them equal to the rest, and concomitantly puts them in an almost aggressive stance against the mainstream society, which considers them to be outcasts and part of a dangerous subculture. Some other *barrio* girls just empathize with the style and look that these gangs project and adopt it.

In this context, this work endeavors to look at the 'other' languages utilized by these three groups of women, and the way these become the conveyors of a certain degree of subversion towards the moral and behavioral mandates of their group and the mainstream community. Or in other words, it intends to observe the way in which these women subvert the established norms and forms through their physical appearance and stance. Acknowledging the fact that the sociocultural situation in which each of these groups developed differs widely, and that their educational chances were, have been and are also different, it is my aim to observe how this other means of communication may serve as a valid tool to gain agency and visibility.

For this purpose, and starting from the premise that clothing, attitude, body language and language itself become part of what I will call personal and communal style, I defend the idea that individual style involves individual agency, and thus ideological meaning. The conclusions arrived at in this work will aim to defend that clothing and body expression is a communicative act, which humans use to "communicate our individuality, and personality, our group and familial associations, our occupations and our status" (Cunningham and Voso Lab 2). In particular, this work will aim to observe the way in which clothing expresses gender and ethnic identification or *disidentification* (Muñoz, J.E.), and may finally serve as a political ideological tool, which supports a structured political agenda in some cases, or becomes a political agenda *per se* in others. With this in mind, as an external-to-the-Mexican/Chicano/a community observer, I will be basing my study on what Lou Taylor denominates an "approach using analysis of photography (and film)" (150), and I align myself with visual sociologist John Grady's idea that "the photographic image is a particularly rich source information that yields much more than mere data. Photographs *do* contain information that can be identified and measured in many different ways; but they are also repositories of meaning that are as puzzling as they are fascinating" (10). For copyright and personal privacy issues, just a few photographs will be included in the work, but the conclusions I reach in it are based in the observation and analysis of a vast array of visual representations that can be found in numerous written and digital resources. Some of these are by anonymous authors, and others, by photographers such as Raul Ruiz, Debra Weber, Joe Razo, Luis C. Garza, Jesus Manuel Mena Garza and María Marquez Sánchez, among many others. Thus, bearing in mind that photographs are representational devices, and may thus – and will be, in fact – interpreted from the viewer's (my own, in this case) perspective, the conclusions arrived at in this work are my own and are aimed at reaching not a generalizing theory, nor do they seek to generalize about a heterogenous, varied and formed-of-individuals community, but a personal reflection on the way the people represented in them communicate through their body, and in particular subvert the norm in a quest for self-definition and a conscious gender, ethnic and class identity articulation. Conscious of the fact that some of the statements that I have included on the role and ideological position of Mexican American men and women may sound categorizing and/or essentializing, especially with regards to issues concerning gender, I find it essential to clarify that these are not group-specific and apply to any society which has developed within the cultural and moral shade of a strong Christian tradition, including my own. In this same line, and before moving on, I would like to state my profound respect to all the women represented in the photographs I include in this work. It is my intention to bring your struggle and your voices to the fore, never to judge you.

Thus, Chapters 1 and 2 introduce some basic notions on the function of dress through Western history and the theoretical grounds upon which I will define the notion of style as a conveyor of meaning and a facilitator of individual agency and give an account of fashion in the 20th century. Chapter 3 dwells on the concept of subcultural groups (and particularly youth subcultural groups) and their relevance for the process of constructing deviant, but nonetheless shared and communal styles. These have helped young people in different sociohistorical times and situations to voice a feeling of nonbelonging to their group or that of the mainstream. In this sense, I will understand the three groups of young women who are the focus of this study to be part of a subculture, as they obviously subvert the moral, behavioral and even physical status quo through their attire and attitude. The next three chapters endeavor to describe the communal style adopted by *Pachucas*, *Chicanas* and *Cholas*. Each of the chapters, in a similar fashion, proposes a general overview of the situation of women in general and women of Mexican American origin in the United States in particular, as well as a general description of the fashion tendencies of each of the particular times in which these three group of women lived. In this context, each chapter proposes that these three collectives formed part of a 'subversive' and transgressive subculture and that their style politics became part of a probably sometimes unconscious, sometimes conscious, act of social subversion.

All in all, the intention of this book is to examine the relevance of clothing, dress and body adornment for the construction of a female personal identity, in an attempt to compare and explain how this means of communication serves as a valid purpose for those women whose political discourse is less articulated than that of those with a clear activist stance. My observations will lead me to the conclusion that those groups whose explicit political agenda was less articulated than others (bearing in mind that both *Pachucas* and *Cholas* have no articulated, defined political agenda in contrast to the *Chicana* activists of the Sixties) adopt a more exaggerated and outwardly defiant style. In this sense, this work aims to show the validity of other languages in portraying and communicating female agency and individuality, and a clear oppositional attitude to established gender and social norms. As this study aims to conclude, an image is sometimes worth a thousand words.

Note

1 Birth rates (live births) per 1,000 females aged 15–19 years for all races.

Chapter 1

Dress, clothing, fashion, and style

Nudity as a natural, inherent human practice was prevalent from prehistoric times until the beginnings of 'modern civilization' in the Western world. Thus, Greek and Roman art and sculpture endeavored to portray and depict mostly male nudes in their most physical, athletic, perfectionist ways. Hair, muscles, hands, feet and genitals were elaborately depicted in the superb representations of the almost-always masculine anatomy that these sculptures presented. These were "youths standing alone, proud and naked. (. . .) The harmonious proportions of the nudes emphasized a balanced whole and communicated grace, strength, and gentleness" (Rubinstein 215). The Bible itself, in Genesis 2:25, observes that "(And) the man and his wife were both naked and were not ashamed." However, there are accounts from anthropological studies of the fact that from the times of the Neanderthal people, they used animal furs to survive and protect their bodies from extreme cold. Clothing was born, and its sole function was that of protecting the human body from the natural elements. The Cro-Magnons continued covering their bodies with furs, and developed more sophisticated garments such as the tunic, as archeological evidence of the fact that they invented the needle to join pieces of fur together suggests ("Prehistoric Clothing").

The progressive civilization of the Western world and subsequent development of norms of conduct and propriety (together with other more physical needs, such as that of protection from cold temperatures) led to the gradual conception of the nude body as shameful, and something that had to be relegated to more intimate spheres and private spaces. The naked body could not be shown in public and its exposure was understood to be disrespectful and obscene. In this sense, getting dressed has become one of the most basic norms of acceptance of social decorum (as well as of a loss of naivety, physicality and, in sum, 'animality.') The Bible, as one of the foundational texts of Western thought and society, clearly established the moral/immoral boundary that provided clothing with a function other than mere physical protection. It says:

> And he said, "I heard the sound of you in the garden, and I was afraid, because I was naked, and I hid myself." He said, "Who told you that you were naked? Have you eaten of the tree of which I commanded you not to eat?"
>
> (Genesis 3:10–11)

According to the text, an act of disobedience brought physicality and prudishness to human beings and, ever since, the need to cover the body has been regarded as a basic condition of the social interaction of humans. Clothes became necessary first for diverse moral and physical reasons, and with the passing of time, they have become markers of social status and/or social adaptation and adaptability. In sociologist Joanne Entwistle's words, "nakedness is wholly inappropriate in almost all social situations" (*Fashioned* 6), and therefore,

> the individual and very personal act of getting dressed is an act of preparing the body for the social world, making it appropriate, acceptable, indeed respectable and possibly even desirable also. (. . .) Dress is the way in which individuals learn to live in their bodies and feel at home in them. (. . .) In this respect, dress is both an intimate experience of the body and a public presentation of it.
>
> (*Fashioned* 7)

Dress historian François Boucher, in fact, highlights some of the functions of clothing, such as inspiring fear and authority, power, rank and/or religious significance. In sum, clothing denotes individual identity within a collective (9–10). Furthermore, he adds that each sociohistorical and political period has seen clothing and costume being adapted and their function changed. It was not until the 14th century that clothing for men and women became different, and it is in this period that we can talk about the birth of fashion and of the "appearance in costume of new elements that owe less to function than to caprice" (Boucher 192). The 16th century Renaissance and the obsession to find beauty were exacerbated by the use of fine materials and luxurious ornaments. The next century, therefore, was characterized by a clear influence of art in costume and clothing, and the influence of French and Dutch fashions was dominant in Europe, mostly among the upper classes and the aristocracy. The development of mechanical production after the Industrial Revolution made clothing change drastically in the 17th century, with the rise of the cotton production, dyes and other materials. But it was after the 19th century, with the emergence of new international trades and the disappearance of the monarchy in France, that styles and modes changed. The middle of the century brought the concept of mass production, and a notable democratization of clothing occurred. World War I, finally, became the turning point, especially in women's costume, for a drastic change in the manners and functions of clothing. Women were 'freer' and more active, and this was, of course, reflected in the way they dressed.

Today, clothes in the Western world have become an extraordinarily popular product of consumption, and the clothing and fashion industries are keystones of the capitalist infrastructure. Not only that, the globalization of the markets has allowed clothes for the First World to be produced in the Third World for Third-World money, thereby widening the gap between the rich and poor countries, the consumer countries and the producers. In sum, the equality expressed in the first human appearance of such a foundational text as the Bible (where the first man and woman were naked and shameless) has turned into the present situation, where clothes are not only regarded as a commodity, but also as a definitory mark of identity.

1.1. The function of dress

Many scholars have led their work towards the definition of the role of clothes and fashion throughout time. Scottish philosopher Thomas Carlyle thought, as early as 1833–34, that the function of clothing was threefold: warmth, decency but mainly, ornamental (1987). No hint yet of the communicative function of clothes. The protective function, obvious to explain the origin of the need to cover oneself, as highlighted by almost all scholars, however, has always been described as complementary to other functions. US scholar and writer Alison Lurie (1992), for instance, underlines the idea of the utility of clothes for protection, just as British psychologist John Carl Flügel had done in 1930. Scholar Elizabeth Rouse (1989) expands the function of the protection of the body, modesty and attraction into a notion essential to our work, which is that of communication. Clothes and personal style communicate. The scholar explains that, however obvious the use of clothing is for protection from nature, for instance, different cultures respond to the same situations in different ways. The cultural side of clothing is thus related to its protective function, just like its second material role: modesty and concealment (Barnard, *Fashion* 53). Rouse and Flügel (1930) continue describing, in their own works, the need for clothing for reasons of decency and morality, concepts based on the heritage of a strong Judeo-Christian tradition. Covering the body, therefore, saves human beings from the same sin that provoked the need for clothing, in Flügel's words. The original sin provided the naked body with a cultural and physical significance that it lacked before the sin, as told in the Genesis. In this regard, the cultural element of clothing is proved to be relevant. For Rouse, moreover, clothing not only serves to avoid shame, but also to distinguish masculine from feminine. Thus, clothing also becomes a marker of gender identity and identification. Following this line, authors such as Roach and Eicher (1979) have debated the connection between clothing and modesty, as to them, modesty is an obvious cultural element. They argue that modesty is not innate to human beings, but that the constant use of clothing has created a particular sense of modesty, and not the other way round. This idea aligns with the notion that "clothing is not the result of modesty, but the cause of modesty; that is, a child is not embarrassed by a lack of clothes until he becomes accustomed to the wearing of clothes" (Horn 4). Finally, clothing may serve the opposite purpose, that is, to attract and exhibit oneself, as pointed out by intellectuals such as Bernard Rudofsky (1947).

Thus, dress was mostly studied in the context of anthropology, until the appearance of cultural studies in the 1960s, without paying any attention to what dressing one way or another implied culturally. Today, contemporary theorists approach dress as a language system, whose main aim is to communicate, and scholars such as Barnard (2002, 2006, 2014), Barthes (1983 (1967)), Eco (1972) and Lurie

(1992) have attempted to define dress and the act of dressing from this viewpoint. However, and according to Entwistle and Wilson, their aims failed to expose the complexities and diversity of the everyday practice of dressing. In contrast to a fixed grammatical language system, as Fred Davis tried to explain in 1992, dress "is more like music than speech, suggestive and ambiguous rather than bound by the precise grammatical rules" (qtd. in Entwistle and Wilson, *Body* 3). In the same vein, Barthes's interesting effort to apply a rhetoric of semiotics with a view to understanding the fashion system failed to address the "many complex social dimensions of fashion as it is practiced in everyday life" (*Body*, 3).

What is obvious for any attempt to study the meaning of dress, or the implications of fashion as a system, is that, for human beings, and for diverse social and physical reasons, getting dressed, and in particular getting dressed in a specific way, is, on the one hand, a need, and on the other, a choice. Kate Soper provides a thorough and interesting review on the way the need for dress has been portrayed in the arts and philosophy in the Western world. The scholar states, first, that according to Virginia Woolf, the need for, and function of dressing was different and meant something different to women and men. For the former, dressing provided a means of creating beauty and attracting men. For men, on the contrary, the way a man dressed implied and demonstrated his social status and relevance (Woolf 176–80, qtd. in Soper 16). The scholar goes on to explain that there are functions of clothing that are not exclusive of human beings, such as covering the body for protection and adornment (just as feathers and fur are), and others that have an aesthetic and semiotic meaning, and are thus exclusive to human beings. In this sense, she explains, "clothes have been very extensively used to assert the cultural status of human beings, to police the border between humans and animals, to deny or cover over our animality and thereby preserve a seemly distance from the beast" (Soper 17). In fact, according to Soper, clothing does not make humans more human, but, as Descartes pointed out, being clothed "is a mark of a distinctively human form of consciousness, of being a 'person'" (92–3, qtd. in Soper 18) and it has an "advertisement function" (Woolf 176, qtd. in Soper 19), which "adheres to the ramifying and complex dress codes which obtain in one's culture" (Soper 19). Or according to Umberto Eco, one speaks through one's clothes (59). Clothing in a certain way, therefore, may imply a sense of human acknowledgment, of a deployment of human dignity and of the acceptance, or otherwise rejection, of a certain social code and system. In fact, and according to Joanne Entwistle, the bond between the body and dress is inextricable, and

> [i]f nakedness is unruly and disruptive, this would seem to indicate that dress is a fundamental aspect of microsocial order. When we dress we do so to make our bodies acceptable to a social situation. (. . .) The body and dress operate dialectically: dress works on the body, imbuing it with social meaning while the body is a dynamic field which gives life and fullness to dress.
> (Entwistle and Wilson, *Body* 35–6)

For the purpose of this work, I would like to pay special attention to what Malcolm Barnard describes as the cultural functions of clothing. First and foremost, one needs to start from the premise that clothing, dressing and fashion are practices of signification, which convey meaning. Clothing creates links among individuals, developing, therefore, a feeling of community (Roach and Eicher 1979; Barnard 2002). Similarly, and interestingly, clothing and the specific individual use of dress serve as a means of individualistic expression (Barnard 2002), which provides each individual with a particular position and space within the previously mentioned community. This community is generally organized in several social layers, and dress and clothing also serve to indicate one's social and even economic status, and therefore one's social role (Barnard 2002). Clothing functions as a marker of political power, of affiliation to a certain religious belief, of participation in social rituals, such as weddings, funerals, etc. or for recreational purposes, such as specific games, etc. In sum, the clothes one chooses are directly related to the external natural forces one lives in, but most of all, clothing implies the position in the group one inhabits and the social norms one would like to respect/subvert. Bearing in mind that clothing and style, as explained by Fred Davis, "do not mean the same things to all members of a society at the same time and that, because of this, what is worn lends itself easily to a symbolic upholding of class and status boundaries in society" (9), it is the aim of this work to dwell upon the boundaries that *Pachucas*, *Chicanas* and *Cholas* aimed to cross and the way the three groups have (or have not) used their clothing choices for this purpose during their specific sociohistorical times. Or, as Diana Crane affirms, to observe the way these women used clothing to "'create(s)' behavior through its capacity to impose social identities and empower people to assert latent social identities" (2).

1.2. Clothing, fashion, and style

Before delving into the matter, a brief pause to explain the meaning and implications of the terms 'fashion' and 'style' would be interesting for my purposes. Fashion, as a category, according to Georg Simmel, is a phenomenon that exists in complex societies, driven by both a "differentiating impulse" and a "socializing one" (546). This definition clearly marks the group, communal essence of fashion, where the different members of different groups ally themselves with a certain group and similarly dissociate themselves from others. Today, and taking into account the growth and relevance of the fashion industry, the term has mainly been reduced to the naming of this industry, which marks the tendencies of a particular time, and is performed and introduced into society by various means, creating what we today call trends.

The term 'fashion,' as objectively defined by the dictionary, implies "a popular way of dressing during a particular time or among a particular group of people" (*Merriam-Webster*) and indicates a collective choice, which is performed consciously or unconsciously, according to the influence of the mandates of the fashion industry. In other words, "a fashion is any style that has gained widespread acceptance in a given period" (Horn 13). In this sense, clothing acts as a cultural agent, as a status marker. Following fashion, the trends of the time, is a means of identification and/or *disidentification* (Muñoz, J.E.) for people, because "fashion is dependent upon the willingness of the majority to conform to it. A number of groups or subcultures refrain from or disdain the current mode in dress. (. . .) Unless one is willing to conform to such standards of simplicity, identification with the group is impossible" (Horn 14). Fashion tendencies have always been present in people's 'choices' regarding clothing (we should bear in mind that the real democratization of fashion and clothing trends did not occur until the late 20th century), and complying with said choices has been interpreted as a symbol of social and cultural position.

According to Simmel (1957 (1904)), at first, fashion was marked by the social elites, and was then imitated by the lower classes, in a hollow attempt to resemble those in socially and culturally superior positions. Clothing became, therefore, following the previous centuries, a clear marker of social class and status and has remained so ever since the 19th century. It became one of the most obvious and apparent markers of social boundaries and class hierarchies. However, things ostensibly changed in the 20th and 21st centuries, and regardless of the fact that there is still a clear-cut division between high-class fashion and clothing (in the form of *haute couture* and luxurious brands) and the most popular forms of fashion and clothing, the democratization of clothing is here with us. Clothing as a consumer good is in the hands of both the elites and the lower classes, and in this sense, the direct identification of clothes and class has been partly erased although there are still a large number of trends and marks that are only eligible for a very specific elite. This, however, does not imply that dress code and clothing tendencies have lost their symbolic meaning. They have, on the contrary, adopted other meanings, in what I will call from now on 'style,' understood as "a particular way in which something is done, created, or performed," "a way of behaving or of doing things" (*Merriam-Webster*) or "a socially or culturally approved way of doing something" (Barnard, *Fashion Theory* 17).

Fashion as a system has been studied by different scholars, but almost- always from a top-down perspective. Thus, Veblen, Simmel and Bourdieu interpret fashion as an indicator of class. This certainly applies to the times when *haute couture* was the axis of the fashion industry. Other theorists such as Blumer, on the other hand, regardless of the fact that they still understand fashion as stemming from the elites, treat it as something that portrays and points towards other emergent trends (Sweetman 62). However, after the several human, social and even economic changes that occurred after the Sixties, fashion as a unitary industry or ideological trend is no longer existent, but is a fragmented *ethos*, which allows for personal performance and choice. In fact, "clothing or dress no longer indexes an external social reality, and particular items, whether fashionable or otherwise, can no longer be said to signify either class, status, or other conventional attributes" (Sweetman 63). It is from this self-driven choice and individuality and from the personal performance of the self within a particular social system and situation that this study departs. However, in many instances, including with the study groups of this work, I align with Paul Sweetman's reading of Maffesoli's notion of an "*empathetic* form of sociality" (68), whereby individuals "lose themselves into a collective subject" (Maffesoli, qtd. in Sweetman, 69), as in the case of the female communities focus of this study. Despite the individual choice regarding the performativity of the body and its communicative capacities, most of the female groups that I will observe, *Pachucas, Chicanas,* and *Cholas,* make this individual choice to *disindividuate* (Maffesoli) themselves and become part of a collective subject that itself performs a particular social position at a particular social time and in a particular social space. Dressing oneself, once again, is an individual act that becomes a collective one in the particular case of homogeneous social groups, subcultures or 'tribes.' Just as, according to Annette Lynch, "normative appearances are most often expressed as individuals strive to fit into their social and cultural context and thus dress to receive positive reviews of their dress from others" (4), and, I would add, to adapt to the norm. Those who deviate, on the other hand, seek to break that same norm and thus express their nonconformity to said norm, and a full alliance with a subcultural one. In this sense, and coming back to the idea of adopting an individual yet collective identity and style through the personal act of dressing, one of the main goals of this book is to understand the way in which the body and dress, together with a particular bodily attitude, become meaningful. Women (and men) of different social status and political awareness have used their bodies and dress attitude/behavior as a means of expressing a particular ideological position. In this sense, the questions posed by Susan Kaiser when she analyzes the relationship between style, truth and subjectivity are valid for this study: "How can I know when I am focused on how I look? To what extent does my appearance create truth(s) about who I am? How do my ways of being, becoming, and appearing interface with those of others?" (79). Or in other words, how does style "as a process or act of managing appearance in everyday life, (. . .) characterize(s) the visible identity construction through which individuals can articulate social psychological yearnings – yearnings that are not only aesthetic but also political in nature"? (80). In this sense, and according to Patrizia Calefato, style, or one's choice to dress,

> immediately displays its semiotic status; it declares, (. . .) then the fact that we are in the presence of a system of intentional signs, with distinctive features, that are discontinuous with regard to a presumed naturalness or hypothetical degree zero of behavior and language. Even when we use expressions like "she has natural style," the contrast between the words "style" and "natural" only serves to highlight the declared unnaturalness of the concept of style.
>
> (27)

The dressing choices of the women in this study thus embody a particular style politics, which itself encompasses a particular adherence to a group ideology.

It is the aim of this book to look at the strategies such groups utilize to convert their bodies into ideological texts, where a political message is inscribed, such as "practices of bodily display and performance associated with dress may be understood as political (although not always contestatory)" (Parkins 2).

According to dress historian Elizabeth Wilson, one of the characteristics of dress is that "it links the biological body to the social being, and public to private. (. . .) It is an organism in culture, a cultural artifact (. . .). Dress is the frontier between the self and the not-self" (2–3). Fashion, for its part, is part of the way we understand dress, and it implies change, it denotes an acceptance or denial of a particular, changing, cultural code of style or even behavior. Although there is evidence of the existence of fashion as a cultural trend even as far back as during the Greek and Roman empires, it was, Wilson states, during the 14th century, when trade grew and cities were established, that fashion as a trend and even an industry started developing towards what it is today. This expansion of commerce brought about a clear growth in the cloth and wool trades, although until the Industrial Revolution fashion was in the hands of the upper classes and the aristocracy. After the revolution and with the growth of cities and a less static class hierarchy, which allowed citizens to move and have a clearer sense of individual choice and identity, clothing acquired different functions according to its purpose. In this sense, clothing not only implied a human need to cover the body, or even a marker of social status, but it also adopted a practical function, and one could already distinguish between clothes for being at home, clothes for public life, etc. In Wilson's terms, gradually "appearance replaced reality" (33), and in the case of women, clothing acquired a very relevant status for the formation of gender roles, as "woman and costumes together created femininity" (29). Moreover, and especially after the 20th century, clothing, in the case of women mostly, represented not only gender but a certain type of personality and thus social stance. For instance, and according to Wilson, in the Twenties, a Los Angeles department store classified its customers into *Romantic, Statuesque, Artistic, Picturesque, Modern* and *Conventional* types (124), and their dress according to these types. Similarly, in 1945, a self-help text for women chose a popular Hollywood star that women could identify with not only in terms of their social attitude but in the way their clothes helped them adopt said attitude. Thus, the manual divided women into *The Exotic, The Outdoor, The Sophisticated, The Womanly, The Aristocrat* or *The Gamine Woman*, and each of these was represented by a film star (124).

However, with the mass consumption of clothes and the functionality and meaning of fashion came also the chance to use dress as a counter-response to the dictates of social mandates. If adopting a certain dress code implied acceptance of different social and gender roles, not following the style or trends of the time also implied a certain social and gender role, as clothes convey meaning and this meaning conveys a social attitude and position. In the case of subcultural groups, they "employ dress to mark out distinctive identities both between themselves and mainstream culture, as well as between themselves and other youth subcultures" (Entwistle, *Fashioned* 135), because "we can use dress to articulate our sense of 'uniqueness,' to express our difference from others, although as members of particular classes and cultures, we are equally likely to find styles of dress that connect us to others as well" (139). And, I would add, dress today is used to express ideological meaning and uniqueness, but similarly, a group's very particular ideological position and, furthermore, ideological uniqueness. In this sense, as will be shown in this volume, the political agenda of women at different historical moments in the United States was clearly expressed by the clothes they chose, or chose not, to wear. Clothes, in fact, and the body they cover have become political texts in the hands of those who have used them, as in the case of the women focused on in this study.

As for the meaning and implications of the term 'style,' taking into account diverse definitions of the term – "a distinctive manner of expression," "a distinctive manner or custom of behaving or conducting oneself," "a particular mode of living," "a particular manner or technique by which something is done, created or performed" (Merriam-Webster online) – I observe that distinctiveness, particularity and individuality are the essence of them all. Or in other words, style refers to the way in which an individual identifies (or *disidentifies*) him/herself with/from others, and delineates his/her own individuality. Dressing style, therefore, refers to the use an individual makes of clothes and fashion to demonstrate his/her social position, his/her degree of acceptance of the social norms, his/her desire to pass or stand out from others and in sum, to become an individual in a global, homogenizing social and cultural infrastructure. As clearly expressed by Diana Crane,

> [c]lothing, as one of the most visible forms of consumption, performs a major role in the social construction of identity. (. . .) One of the most visible markers of social status and gender and therefore useful in maintaining or subverting symbolic boundaries, clothing is an indication of how people in different eras have perceived their positions in social structures and negotiated status boundaries. (. . .) Clothes as artifacts "create" behavior through their capacity to impose social identities and empower people to assert latent social identities.
>
> (1–2)

According to Crane, then, clothing is an active agent in the construction of the modern persona, and thus getting dressed becomes a political act. In this sense, modern individuals shape their social identities in general, or at particular moments in their social agenda, by means of the clothes they wear, and, traditionally, in the case of women, by means of the makeup and hairstyle they choose. It is particularly clear also that, taking into account the previously mentioned democratization of clothing choices and the blurring of class boundaries as a consequence of such choices, individual style becomes symbolic of individual agency. Regardless of the obvious existence of dress codes for particular situations (work, celebrations, casual meetings, sports events, etc.), it is in the hands of each individual to conform to the norms or, on the contrary, subvert them and create his/her own, self-conscious style.

In this context, breaking the norms of conduct, propriety and behavior that clothing implies has become, through the different ages and eras, one of the most obviously subversive means of contestation. Clothing, as one of the first visible physical components of a socialized human body, has acquired a strong meaning in recent decades, especially after the countercultural movements of the Sixties. The female collectives focused on in this study, in fact, are representative of women who chose to deviate (or who deviated in a nonconscious way) from the norm, and used clothes and other elements of body language (style) as a site of contest and rebellion. Clothes, makeup, speech and body attitude acquire meaning (are given meaning), and become symbols of an urgent need, sometimes, to shatter the norms, and most of the time to express individual choice and agency. As we will see in the following pages, the aims and results of adopting a certain style may vary among the different collectives, historical periods, social contexts, etc., but style and the individual choice of style always conveys an inextricable meaning. Moreover, a 'different' style is conceived with the purpose of creating this counter, opposing meaning, as explained by Dick Hedbige:

> Style in subculture is, then, pregnant with significance. Its transformations go "against nature," interrupting the process of "normalization." As such, they are gestures, movements towards a speech which offends the "silent majority," which challenges the principle of unity and cohesion, which contradicts the myth of consensus.
>
> (18)

I would add to his words that most of the time style not only interrupts the process of normalization, but it provokes this interruption. Hence, a subversive style politics could well be regarded as one of the most politically radical stances ever. In the case of women, whose social and moral conduct has been forever determined by religious, social and gender (in sum, political and ideological) issues, adopting a deviant style and body language becomes an extraordinarily political act – in most cases, therefore, an act that is punished and condemned by the 'silent majority' it profoundly offends. When individuals rebel against the norm and become a deviant group, a natural process of 'otherization' and marginalization from the mainstream occurs. This invokes fear and mistrust on the part of the majority, which feels attacked and thus aims to stereotype and ostracize the rebellious group. In the case of Mexican American women, in particular, breaking the patriarchal norm through 'indecent' acts and means of expression becomes one of the most severe affronts women could inflict on their community. The intricate and complex sociocultural history of this group shows the (probably inevitable and necessary) ability to adapt, amalgamate and change that this collective has had after centuries of colonization, occupation, linguistic, religious and cultural conversion, war and revolution, to name just a few sociohistorical situations. However, the gender division of the group, maintained and transmitted through an extended mythology and religious imagery, has favored a total impermeability with regard to female agency and individual choice. The changes that Mexican American women have gone through, both in their social agenda and in their individual choices, are inscribed in the clothes they wear, which concomitantly define their identity. Moreover, as I will point out in this book, the clothing these women chose to wear at each of these specific sociohistorical times may well be considered the catalysts of these changes, as it was through clothing and physical appearance that they demonstrated their uneasiness with the status quo. Joan Entwistle affirms that "fashion responds to social and political changes, reflecting and reproducing these changes" (80, qtd. in Barnard 2002). I would add that in many cases, the way one uses fashion and/or anti-fashion may provoke said changes.

In the particular case of the women focused on in this study, and especially the *Pachucas*, their conscious particular use of clothing and physical appearance turned them and their male counterparts into part of a subcultural movement that was understood by many as an affront to mainstream society. This attire, overall physical appearance and attitude 'otherized' them and situated them in a position of marginality within the group, which pointed towards them as betrayers. Their look, which obviously expressed deviation, is understood as a drastic rejection of the norms and traditions of the community, which, in the case of women, are regarded as intrinsic to their female nature. However, their probably unconscious use of their clothes as a means of contesting their tradition and the established gender roles designed for them turned them into 'passive political activists,' and thus precursors of the *Chicana* feminist movement. In the case of the members of the Movement, who defended a clear political stance, which vindicated their rights as *Chicanas* and as women, their choice of clothes was part of their political agenda, and represented an act of rebellion against the gender roles of the times. Similarly, it aligned these women with other ongoing movements (feminist, hippie, etc.), creating a sense of group identification among them all. The case of the 20th century *Cholas* is far more similar to the first *Pachucas*, as, lacking a clearly elaborated political discourse, their clothing joins them together as part of a group, and similarly provides them with a differentiating style in relation to the mainstream group. The following pages will be aimed at showing how clothing and physical appearance have been used as tools of contestation for these women, and how style has facilitated the acquisition of their visibility in different sociohistorical periods.

Aligning myself with the idea of the intimate relationship between the body and dress, social codes and their acceptance or rejection, it is the aim of this volume to address the way in which women of Mexican American origin in the United States have demonstrated their subjectivities as individuals and members of a group by means of the utilization of both body and dress and language as a communication system. The study will observe the means by which the existence of an articulated system of political and ideological thought and discourse (or its absence) has provided the grounds for the body and dress to be used as tools of communication and, in this case, as markers of belonging or nonbelonging to a particular group. As Entwistle reflects on the work of French philosopher Merleau-Ponty, for whom the self is located within the body, and this itself is embodied in a particular manner at a particular time and in a particular space, "dress is always located spatially and temporarily: when getting dressed one orientates oneself/ one's body to the situation, acting in a particular way. (. . .) Thus the dressed body is not a passive object, acted upon by social forces, but actively produced through particular, routine and mundane practices" (*Body* 45–6). Dressing in a particular way in a particular situation at a particular moment is a performative individual practice, which renders meaning to the acceptance or rejection of the social norms the body and the self are required to fulfill. Through dress, the individual thus demonstrates an agentic social position and renders his/her body meaningful and communicative. In sum, the intention of this book is to observe the way in which women of Mexican origin in the United States, and at very particular sociohistorical moments, have sought personal and communal agency through their personal (and group) 'style.' Before going any further, I think it is relevant to state that, for my purpose, I understand style as an individual choice made by women in this case that conveys a particular personal image with a specific purpose. Style thus implies not only clothing but adornment, makeup, hairstyle, body language and even parlance and acts and attitudes that in a way create and shape an identity (or a representation of a given identity). Personal style thus fulfills a particular function, and conveys a personal choice to express oneself.

Chapter 2

The 20th century and fashion

The 20th century was undoubtedly the time when fashion as a mass concept grew to the extent that we know it nowadays. The industrialization of dress production, the democratization of the fashion industry, the developments in technology in the garment industry and the mass outreach of fashion publicity by means of fashion magazines, or even the film industry, led to the expansion of the fashion business in general, and individual choice for dress in particular. However, it is also true that dress and fashion, or style in general, have always been marked by the sociopolitical agendas of a particular time in a particular space, and in the case of women's fashion and dress codes, diverse historical moments have marked the different dress choices of women.

In the Forties, a time of war and austerity, women's fashion was marked not only by the political and economic situation of the country at the time, but also by the general moral mood of the nation, which called for sobriety and propriety. Before the War, France (Paris) had already become the fashion mirror, but after the occupation of Paris during the War, the French fashion industry was brought to a halt. For this reason, in the United States, the British look became more popular. This defined the tendency for women to dress in a uniform-like style, and to show clean, bare faces, which denoted decency and austerity. According to *Fashion Illustrated* magazine, "the woman who could change instantly into service clothes or munitions overalls and look charming, *soignée*, and *right* is the smart woman of today" (Batterberry 330). In the same way, women changed to wearing trousers as they entered the heavy-industry workforce. This was probably the greatest change in the understanding of women's fashion and women's gender and social roles. The adoption of trousers was mostly due to their functionality and comfort as work attire. For some, however, the idea that the adoption of pants by women was a big step in their liberation is, to say the least, not totally true. Elizabeth Wilson points out that for many, and especially from a feminist viewpoint, women have "made progress in the public sphere of paid work, [but] (*my brackets*) this has been on male terms and within the parameter of masculine values" (165). Notwithstanding its connotations, one cannot deny that the normalization of trousers for women meant a change in the lives of women in the Forties, in spite of the fact that this was in a way 'forced' by the socioeconomic situation of the times. The

"Eisenhower jacket"[1] (with "roomy shoulders and pockets" (Batterberry 331)) also became a must in the lives of women in the Forties. Skirts were shorter than before and showing the legs was partly regarded as a patriotic act and even duty, "something for the boys" (Batterberry 331).

The scarcity and austerity provoked by the War years also brought changes to the fashion industry and designers had to adapt to the new materials that existed in this new, sober reality. Synthetic materials were designed to replace wool, and were manufactured in colors such as "Flag Red" and "Victory Blue" both in the United States and Great Britain (Batterberry 333). These were, however, good years for American designers, who, having not received any feedback from the previously strong French fashion industry, could develop an 'American look,' which responded to the demands of the country during the War years. Among these designers, the work of Claire McCardell should be highlighted, as her "list of innovations is endless: double stitching, visible hardware closings (including her favorite brass hooks), the strapless elasticized 'tube' top, the dirndl, the diaper bathing suit, the wrap-around coverall, dress, and a variety of winter play clothes" (Batterberry 342). Regardless of the styles and materials, McCardell praised herself for being a patriotic designer, whose inspiration was always American: "It's freedom, it's democracy, it's casualness, it's good health. Clothes can say all that" (Batterberry 342).

However, the lives of ordinary women were far removed from those exposed in *Vogue* or *Harper's Bazaar*, and many designers found inspiration in more "common girls," represented by singers who acted in musicals to "cheer up the boys," such as Lana Turner, Dorothy Lamour and Veronica Lake. Michael and Ariane Batterberry describe them as wearing "a sweater, a sarong and crimson-red lips" (347). In a similar manner, women and femininity were demonstrated in the shape of the "pinup girl" who, "while bosomy, had an otherwise boyish figure with narrow waist and hips and small buttocks. Her hair was vampishly long or swept up in flirtatious curls on top of her head" (Batterberry 347). The genderization and sexualization of this image is obvious, and lived together with the working woman in the pants, the sober "world of the padded shoulders, tight waists, and short skirts, of privation and makeshifts" (Batterberry 347).

The end of the War brought few changes in the everyday choices of women for clothing, but in the world of *haute couture* and fashion, a change *was* happening. Christian Dior, who emerged as the symbol of the French fashion world after the War, created what was called "The New Look," which consisted of "rounded shoulders, full bust, nipped waist, padded hips and long, sweeping skirt, supported by petticoats, high heels and ankle straps" (Batterberry 349). The Dioran look provoked a strong reaction from many women, who thought, on the one hand, that taking the skirts back down was a step too far in the liberation of the female body, due to "its overt and lascivious sensuality and its entrapment of women as objects of desire and decoration" (Breward 191), and on the other, that it was an indecent moral patriotic act, as there was still a scarcity of materials and clothes. In contemporary terms, the existentialist ideology of Sartre and Camus, and the feminism of De Beauvoir were paving the way for a new aesthetics and a radical new conception of the place of human beings in the world. Their ideological, political and social stance was demonstrated by means of "assuming a deliberately disheveled appearance as an expectoration in the face of 'fashion.' (. . .) They preferred 'modern' déshabillé – a loose sweater and pants for men and women alike" (Batterberry 353).

Two decades later, the sons and daughters of the men and women who fought the War and defended the home front, maintaining their households and factories, part of the baby boom after the War, were already adolescents who would soon enter the consumption society. A new social group was emerging: the teenagers, who were numerous, and potentially powerful in terms of capitalist consumption and active participation in society. The gender roles expected for boys and girls started to gradually be questioned, and the girls who went to colleges had no interest in creating a safe home that they could decorate, but rather spent their money on "travel, education, records, high-fidelity equipment and, above all, clothing" (Batterberry 366). The countercultural young generation of the Sixties identified themselves as hippies, and Charles Reich (qtd. in Batterberry) defines this young community's relationship with clothes in the following terms: "[T]heir clothing expresses wholeness of self. There is no schizophrenic division between dress for the office and dress for play. No individual is limited by this clothing to a role" (366). Long hair, long skirts, bare feet, and a mixture of oriental adornments and/or garments from other decades became just a few of the possible combinations that the free youth could use to express themselves through clothing. Denim pants became a symbol of unisex clothing, and embodied a democratization of clothing, as well as a challenge to the establishment. Similarly, and together with the sexual revolution, the youth of the Sixties sought a return to the 'lost paradise' to fulfill the arcadian dream, and nudity was embraced as a valid means of ideological communal and self-expression. Elizabeth Wilson describes the naturalistic, Thoreauan, Whitmanistic hippie style in the following manner:

> Hair, which had been short, lacquered and straight, became long and curly, for both sexes. Sleeves which had been tight and shortish became long, gathered, flowing. Bell-bottomed trousers widened until they looked like skirts, and skirts which had been short and straight sank to the floor. Jackets were suddenly flowery, eighteenth century, and brocade and velvet bloomed. Scarves, a garment unknown either to the mods or Mary Quant, were festooned in twos, threes, fours around the throat, to sink floating to the knees. Collars got larger and longer, like rabbits ears. Makeup became first naturalistic, then vampishly exaggerated as Biba popularized the thirties style.
> (192)

Needless to say, the Sixties fashion was, for many, the great revolution in the step towards the demand for individual choice in all walks of life. The hippie attire, which was regarded as free, natural and connected to earth, was, without doubt, a liberating one, a call for individual freedom, but at the same time it represented a symbol of identification with a particular group and a particular and very specific ideological position. In this sense, the hippie style conveyed a strong ideological meaning and the individual choice of adopting such a style demonstrated an oppositional attitude to the prevalent status quo in the Sixties and Seventies: the hippie attire expressed a nonviolent attitude to life, a free understanding of human sexuality and gender relationships, a desire to experiment with drugs and, in sum, a rejection of capitalism and its constraining ideological implications. The hippie attire can be considered what Wilson calls "oppositional dress" (203) or "oppositional style," which "attempt(s) to subvert dominant ideologies, using the very mass consumption means that constitute and contribute to the ideologies" (204). Or in other words, the hippie style was soon adopted by the mainstream and commodified as a consumption product. However, it is also undeniable that its meaning and semiotic power was exceptional.

The Sixties and Seventies paved the way for the acquisition of a politically active attitude on the part of many young people in the Western world, which was often expressed by their clothes and body language, parlance and attitude. Music became a means of cohering many of the emerging 'urban tribes or subcultures,' which were often a physical exponent of young people's dissatisfaction with the status quo. Similarly, however, these young people were also the target of a fierce and emerging consumerist trend aimed directly at them. In sum, the turbulent but very creative Sixties and Seventies became the beginning of a new era for the youth of the day, who ironically took part in cohesive music, fashion and ideological groups, but adopted from then on a more individualized attitude towards clothing and personal expression and identity.

The ensuing decades, marked by an obvious cultural and economic predominance of the United States in the Western world, were diverse and individualistic in terms of fashion, clothing and style. The emergence of a very powerful leisure industry, where music, television and cinema became products of mass consumption, marked the fashion trends among people in general, and young people in particular. Pop singers such as Madonna and Michael Jackson became fashion icons for a generation, and as an abundance of 'ready-to-wear' businesses emerged and grew extensively, young people opted for their style choices in an individual way. This choice aligned oneself with either a musical trend, an ideological position or a socioeconomic status. Similarly encouraged by the popular mass media and its icons, an openness to sexuality, praise for health and body care and an obvious opting for comfort marked people's (especially young people's) choices regarding dress.

In sum, 20th century fashion paved the way for the democratization of fashion and clothing alternatives, as well for a gradual acquisition of agency and individual choice. Similarly, and yet contrastingly, it was also the century of the emergence of young people as an economically and politically active social collective. Many of these youngsters identified with the mainstream ideological and aesthetic trends of each of the decades. Others, on the other hand, did not feel at ease with the normative trends of the times, and created what have been labeled as 'subcultures,' which were mostly demonstrated through the display of a different aesthetic, and a 'contesting' style. These subcultures emerged mostly after World War II, and marked the essence of a young generation that could be seen and heard within the still uniform diverse mainstream styles and fashion trends that were popular in the 20th century. In contrast to this, the young generation of the first decades of the 21st century are engulfed in a massive and blurring globalizing cultural reality, which shows that difference and divergence are not so easily recognized and visualized within an ironically more individualistic and heterogeneous but similarly very globalized and homogeneous reality. All attempts at difference and subversion are quickly melded into the mainstream globalized world and turned into sellable goods and trends, and young people find it more difficult to stand out in their rebellion through their physical look and attitude. The 20th century, in contrast, was a time of revolutions, where rebellious and idealistic young people believed in change and used their bodies to demonstrate how such change could be brought about.

Note

1 "[A] short jacket fitting snugly at the waist and cuffs; one used as a part of a military uniform." (Merriam-Webster.com)

Chapter 3

Style, subcultures, and Mexican American women

The efforts to define what a subculture is have been many and varied, but we can go back to the year 1947, when sociologist M.M. Gordon defined subcultural groups as "smaller 'pieces' of a larger culture or society, differing in some way from 'mainstream' culture" (qtd. in Haenfler, 15). Regardless of the wide and even generalizing essence of this definition, when studying the existence of these little pieces within the big cake, we cannot forget that subcultural groups, 'deviant' groups, are, like other kinds of collectives, heterogeneous, ever-changing groups that evolve over time and are in constant contact with other social forces. Ross Haenfler, for his part, proposes the following, more contemporary definition: "a relatively diffuse social network having a shared identity, distinctive meanings around certain ideas, practices, and objects, and a sense of marginalization for or resistance to a perceived 'conventional' society" (16). This definition seems more appropriate than the first one, and it includes the notion of a changing group, which shares symbols, objects and ideas, and somehow deviates from the norm. Taking this more inclusive approach into account, we can then suggest that the three target groups of this study can be considered subcultural, in the sense that they somehow 'deviate' from the cultural, gender and attitudinal norms established by the communities in their particular sociohistorical moments. *Pachucas*, *Chicanas* and *Cholas* are/were probably not conscious participants of a given 'subcultural' group *per se*, but one cannot deny the fact that the three groups represent and demonstrate some kind of deviance from the mainstream and their community's roles in terms of behavior and moral codes. Ken Gelder, for his part, defines subcultural identity as "something formulated away from home and family but which compensates for this lack by organizing new, alternative kinds of sociality, however they might be described" (18). For him, "very few subcultures have widespread social change on their agenda, nor (with some exceptions) do they imagine that society's values ought somehow to reflect or absorb their own" (22). Gelder's definition of subculture will serve me as the theoretical starting point for this work, which is aimed at drawing interpretative conclusions regarding whether the target groups of this study had a clear and elaborate political agenda and the way they demonstrated this through their dress style, body language and general attitude, or instead, whether their dress style, body language and attitude became their political agenda *per se*.

The observation of 'deviant' young people and their labeling as 'subcultural' was first developed at the University of Chicago, which was home to one of the first sociology departments in the country. Chicago School scholars Shaw and McKay, who studied crime and deviance in the city at the beginning and in the middle of the century, pointed out as early as in 1942 that "deviance was a symptom of rapid progress, especially the inequality produced by rapid social change" (Haenfler 4). Others, in the early 1920s, such as Robert Park and Ernest W. Burgess, had already defended the idea that "rapid migration, industrialization, political upheaval, technological innovation, and economic change" (Haenfler 4) bring "social disorganization," which similarly provokes deviance and conflict. This theory is still maintained today, and the role of the social environment in the generation of trouble and defiance is highlighted as the primary source of this deviance. Other scholars have added nuances to this notion: for instance, in 1963 Howard Becker pointed out the relevance of labeling for identifying these groups as deviant (Haenfler 4). They became deviant once others considered and thus labeled them so, and they were stigmatized (Goffman 1963) forever. In the following decades, the Center for Contemporary Cultural Studies (CCCS) of the University of Birmingham, which was adhered to the New Left, posited that social class was the main reason why youth groups became deviant in the face of the cultural hegemony (Gramsci 1971) imposed by the capitalist society. Dick Hebdige's groundbreaking *Subculture: The Meaning of Style* talked about subcultural style as a form of *bricolage* (Haenfler 8) that created a kind of "homology" (9), a kind of homogeneous, synergic tendency among its members, making them both deviants and adherents to a certain norm. For CCCS scholars, therefore, subcultural groups are a product of class divisions, they adopt defiant styles that convey a meaning of resistance, and as a consequence, the mainstream reacts against them, creating a feeling of "moral panic" around them (Cohen 2002 (1972)). Haenfler elaborates on the notion of moral panic coined by Cohen, and describes the reaction subcultures create among the mainstream society in the terms that Goode and Ben-Yahuda used in 1994 as "concern, hostility, consensus, disproportionality and volatility" (105). These stages were generally performed and created by the people in general, or interest groups, such as politicians, religious leaders or the media. According to Haenfler, Cohen described the role the media has in the creation of moral panic against these groups: they generally exaggerate and distort the image of the group, creating a strong, simplistic process of symbolization of its members that would be easily recognizable by the population. This occurred undoubtedly in the case of the Zoot Suit Riots, where the Los Angeles media gave an almost caricaturesque image of the zoot suiters, as we will see in the following chapters.

The study of girls within the subcultural groups was addressed by Angela McRobbie and Jenny Garber in an essay that appeared in the volume by Stuart Hall and Tony Jefferson, *Resistance Through Rituals* (1975). They pointed out that the term "subculture" itself was very masculinist. In their essay, they explained the fact that girls had been kept invisible in their bedrooms, as well as the fact that they had often been the target of consumerism rather than of any "ritual of resistance" (96). All these features well may be applied to the three groups that will be analyzed in the following pages. *Pachucas*, *Chicanas* and *Cholas*, as members of communities that have been traditionally considered inferior and second class in the sociocultural arrangement of the US, have not only been kept in their bedrooms in the most literal sense of the word, but also in the figurative 'bedroom' of the social and cultural life of the nation. Their obvious second-class citizenry and their, in many cases, lower educational opportunities have deprived them of a reality that positioned them in the mainstream culture. In this sense, the women who are the focus of this study not only belong to an ethnic subculture (as understood as a little part of the big socioeconomic and cultural panorama), but similarly, they have always been part of a subculture within their own subculture, as women who, in McRobbie's terms, were kept in their bedrooms. And moreover, the women who are the focus of this study, who dared defy the governing rules and traditions within their group, formed a new subculture within, which consciously or unconsciously subverted these rules and traditions. In the particular case of women of Mexican American origin in the United States of the 20th century, the metaphorical space of their bedroom had diverse layers, formed by rules of behavior and conduct that arose both from their community and from that of the mainstream. When these women dared open the doors of their bedrooms and looked out, but mostly dared show themselves, the sense of moral panic that they created was very powerful. On the one hand, this was because their own community and cultural tradition never expected these women to defy said tradition. The strong and deeply assimilated gender roles that they had interiorized as natural to their existence seemed forever unquestionable and part of their inherent destiny. On the other hand, for the mainstream group, these women were invisible and nonexistent, and as soon as they left their bedrooms and dared cross the physical borders that the hierarchical ethnic arrangement of the country imposed, they were seen as dangerous. The very fierce attempt to otherize and criminalize them soon turned them into social deviants and thus doomed them to conceptual and real persecution. In Neil Campbell's words, America, considering itself to be a young country that was created as a rejection of the parent culture of the Old World (2), has always been enthralled by the creation of youth narratives. However, it also regards them with fear and suspicion when "other 'excluded' groups intervene, such as women, *Chicanos/as* of African-Americans, to produce and circulate their own stories of youth which may run counter to the mainstream, but which utilize certain patterns in youth representation to promote particular notions of community or serve other political purposes" (2).

However, and from a more objective viewpoint, regardless of the fact that the female collectives who are the focus of this study have lived different sociocultural and economic situations, and that the span of time that separates them is about five decades, it is also true that they all share some similarities regarding their position both in the arrangement of the mainstream society and within their own groups. In all cases, these women have been revolutionary for their times, and theirs has been a struggle for self-recognition and individual agency. The three collectives that will form the thematic core of this book are women who, by means of their personal and physical bodily attitudes, have become deviant and subversive. *Pachucas*, hence, were protagonists of a silent revolution, and their attitude and attire became an affront to normality, both for the 'normative' Anglo-Saxon social community and for their own group, who considered them different and dangerous. Their different and thus dangerous and aggressive attire and physical and bodily stance turned them into betrayers of their group. However, this study will show that theirs was not a consciously organized revolution, but they were women who felt, just as the males of their subgroup, the *Pachucos*, not at ease with what society in general, and their community in particular, offered them. In the very particular case of *Pachucas*, servitude, docility, submission and an extremely limited education was considered their natural fate and future. *Pachucas* rejected this future and their overt, physical revolution and defiant attitude and style became revolutionary and planted the seeds for the forthcoming politically very engaged community, the *Chicanas*.

Two decades later, *Chicanas*, or women who were sympathetic to the *Chicano* movement, *La Causa*, and became conscious political activists, adopted an overtly more politically sophisticated and elaborate stance, which was also accompanied by a 'different to the norm' way of acting, dressing and, in sum, expressing oneself through one's body. These women, conscious of the plight of women in general and the women of their ethnic and cultural community in particular, in regard to agency, a voice and a life of one's own, defied their group and the mainstream behavioral gender mandates through both their voice and their bodies. The struggle for sexual liberation was overtly political, and, in contrast to their forebears (the *Pachucas*), the *Chicana* activists shared and developed a well-structured political agenda. Among their gender-based demands, the *Chicana* activists struggled for cultural and social recognition and their cultural and political plight vindicated their indigenous social and ethnic heritage, which put them in a different position within the ethnocultural mainstream US panorama. *Chicanas*, as opposed to *Pachucas* and the contemporary *Cholas*, in this sense, added the notion of ethnic identity, a factor that in many instances is not contemplated in the definitions of subculture provided in the previous pages. Many of the approaches to youth subcultures that have been described seem not to include the concept of ethnicity and consider subcultural groups as being directly related to class only. In fact, Stuart Hall, when describing the oppositional nature of said groups, asserts that they fight in an imaginary way, as they are never able to solve their class and occupation problems. In the case of women of Mexican origin, and very particularly in that of the overtly political *Chicanas* of the Sixties, the issue of ethnicity appeared to be directly linked to that of class and the, of course, core aspect of their struggle, gender. In this regard, *Chicanas* of the Sixties epitomized the notion that Hall discusses of the double nature of subcultural groups, and especially of those of young people. *Chicanas*, oppositional and revolutionary as they were, defended their sociocultural and ethnic belonging to a very particular community in the United States, that of Mexican Americans. They opposed both their community for what its cultural traditions imposed on them in terms of gender roles and fought for the acceptance and valuation of their cultural specificity and value. According to Clarke, Hall Jefferson and Roberts, thus,

> Members of a sub-culture may walk, talk, act, look "different" from their parents and from some of their peers, but they belong to the same families, go the same schools, work at much the same jobs, live down the same "mean streets" as their peers and parents. In certain crucial respects, they share the same position (vis-à-vis the dominant culture), the same fundamental and determining life-experiences, as the "parent" culture from which they derive. Through dress, activities, leisure pursuits and life-style, they may project a different cultural response or "solution" to the problems by their material and social class position and experience. But the membership of a sub-culture cannot protect them from the determining matrix of experiences and conditions which shape the life of their class as a whole. They experience and respond to the same basic problematic as other members of their class who are not so differentiated and distinctive in a "subcultural" sense. Especially in relation to the dominant culture, their sub-culture remains like other elements in their class culture – subordinate and subordinated.
>
> (8)

In this respect, the *Chicana* activists' stance, oppositional and deviant as it was, responded to what Hall defines as a subcultural group's 'double articulation' as it deviates and at the same time adheres to the norm. In the case of the *Chicanas* of the Sixties, this double articulation became obviously complex, as their deviance was targeted not only at the mainstream, dominant US group but also at their own one, which was too traditional and oppressive towards women. Similarly, their male peers' obvious lack of empathy and understanding of their plight also made them subgroupal to the *Chicano* male activists, with whom, similarly, they shared a lot of demands. Finally, the *Chicana* feminists of the Sixties created a bond with the white feminists of the times, with whom they shared the gender-based essential issues of their flight, but with whom they did not coincide in terms of the relevance of class and race in the specificity of the women's discriminated against situation. Similarly, the hippie movement, the hippie subculture, was part of the big sociocultural scenario in which the *Chicanas*' fight occurred. Undoubtedly, their sociocultural and political position was manifold and, needless to say, oppositional and revolutionary.

Finally, *Cholas*, or *barrio* girls (not always necessarily linked to the gang system), also respond to the definitions and concepts regarding subculture that have been pointed out so far. *Cholas* in the Nineties, characterized in very general terms as being part of a low class, and many times as not having been able to acquire a good education, and thus proper occupational and professional chances, form part of the vast array of contemporary youth subcultural groups. These women, as part of a group not only discriminated against but deprived of all mainstream sociocultural and economic chances, react to both the mainstream and their own community in a probably not very politically conscious way, but, among many other means, through their style, attire and life attitude in general.

What is clear when observing the social attitude of these three groups of women is that part of their oppositional stance towards both the dominant community and their own group is that they demonstrate this opposition in a more or less conscious way, through the nonconventional style and attitude that they adopt. According to J. Patrick Williams, "style and subculture go hand in hand" (67). Yet,

> style is more than clothing; more than surface imagery. Style is active, performed, and practiced; produced by people in everyday situations. Subculturalists create new forms of demeanor, behavior, or talk, just as they create new clothing, art, or music. Style depicts much more than an impotent "class consciousness": it represents the self-consciousness of its creator in both an individualistic and collective sense.
>
> (75)

According to Williams, therefore, style is a self-conscious intentional reaction that implies a relationship between one's self-conscious image and an ideology. In his words, this relationship may be understood by the concept of homology, which was defined by Clarke in the year 1976 and addresses the fact that one's style "must have the 'objective possibility' of reflecting the particular values and concerns of the group" (qtd. in Williams, 75). Therefore, this volume will address the way the three groups of girls' styles have this objective possibility or are, to say the least, intentional. Starting from the premise that the sociocultural, economic and even historical situation of these three collectives differs significantly from one another and that each of them demonstrated a different position towards their own community and the mainstream one, I defend the idea that the three groups presented a certain degree of opposition, both to their group and society in general. Hence, and assuming that style and body attitude are part of the cultural means of signification of an individual or a group, the style these three groups of women adopted, or adopt, created, or creates, both cohesion among themselves and disjunction from their group and the mainstream one. In Mike Brake's words, they create new

> meaning systems, modes of expression or life styles developed by groups in subordinate structural positions in response to dominant meaning systems, and which reflect their attempt to solve structural contradictions arising from the wider societal context. As such, a subculture has to develop new group meanings, and an essential aspect of its existence is that it forms a constellation of behavior, action and values which have meaningful symbolism for the actors involved.
>
> (9)

These new meanings and symbols are in most cases embodied through the adoption of a very particular oppositional or deviant style, through which these collectives adhere to each other and break with the normative mandates, or adopt what Glaser calls "differential identification" (qtd. in Brake). This identification is not only demonstrated through dress but is part of a wider code of look and behavior. In Brake's stance, a deviant style is demonstrated by "image," "demeanor" and "argot" (12), which together perform a clearly deviant and oppositional attitude and style. Following Brake's notion of style, this "is used for a variety of meanings. It indicates which symbolic group one belongs to, it demarcates that group from the mainstream, and it makes an appeal to an identity outside that of a class-ascribed one" (13). Thus, subcultural groups, or deviant groups, demonstrate what John Clarke and others denominate "*bricolage*," using the Levi-Strauss notion, whereby "the bricoleur re-locates the significant object in a different position within that discourse, using the same overall repertoire of signs, or when the object is placed within a different total ensemble, a new discourse is constituted, a different message conveyed" (Clarke, "Style" 149). This style, this attempt at *bricolage*, creates "agency through fragmentation" (Hall). It is the purpose of this volume to elucidate the intentionality and means of the creation of agency by these three diverse collectives of women.

In many cases, as previously stated, most of the studies that have been devoted to the study of subculture have left women on one side. The aim here is to observe whether these girls, not openly acknowledged in the literature regarding youth subcultural groups, are really absent, passively present or rendered invisible for the observers and theorists of these groups. In Angela McRobbie and Jenny Garber's words,

> It may be, however, that the marginality of girls is not the best way of representing their position in the sub-cultures. The position of the girls may be, not marginally, but structurally different. They may be marginal to the subcultures, not simply because girls are pushed by the dominance of males to the margin of each social activity, but because they are centrally into a different, necessarily subordinate set or range of activities. Such an analysis would depend not on their marginality but on their structured secondariness.
>
> (179)

In this same context, and following the notion of the triple discrimination articulated by *Chicana* feminists during the Sixties, the situation of *Chicana* women, who are, moreover, part of a subcultural group, becomes extremely complicated, as their opposition to the norm is manifold and their "differential identification" is shaped facing diverse and in most cases noncomplementary communities. Thus, *Pachucas* of the Forties were women of a low class and a negatively marked ethnic origin within the overall mainstream social organization, but were also marked by the role of gender in an overtly patriarchal community. Finally, their *Pachuca* attitude, style, argot and demeanor were considered an affront by both the mainstream society and their own group, who considered them deviant women, and thus betrayers of their group and traditions.

Chicanas of the Sixties, with their more articulated political discourse, a higher education and a supposedly more elaborate social and personal agenda, were also considered deviant by both the mainstream community (although they adhered to the feminist and hippie movements of the times, which were themselves regarded as deviant), and their group, who thought their vindications were a direct and grave betrayal of their group.

Finally, low-class girls of the urban *barrios* in the Nineties, when they joined or lived around the gang system, in many cases as a means of survival, also demonstrated a deviant position in relation to their group on the one hand, and the normative, mainstream rule on the other, and their style, demeanor and argot became clearly oppositional and differential.

In the following pages, I will aim to describe these particular styles and observe the degree of intentionality these women demonstrated. In the same way, I will aim to conclude whether an oppositional attitude has any direct relationship with a conscious political opposition or deviation from the norm, or if these girls embody what I will from now on call an act of *subversion and deviation through the (un)conscious.*

Chapter 4

Pachucas

Breaking the norm in the Forties

4.1. Life and expectations for US women in the Forties

World War II was, without doubt, the sociopolitical event that marked all spheres of the course of life in the Forties, both for men and women. The country became involved in the War in 1942, and everything changed in the daily lives of Americans. Men (or the majority of the young, productive men in the country) joined the armed forces and left the country in a highly patriotic effort (there were an estimated 16.1 million troops involved in the conflict (World War II)). Women remained in the country, and their endeavors and tasks on the home front also became a highly patriotic effort of a different nature.

Theirs was the job of 'looking after the country,' the homes and the kids, but, with the spectacular increase in the demand for arms, the number of factories devoted to manufacturing these arms grew enormously. This production required workers who could make the arms, and women found a chance (and a challenge) to enter the workforce outside their homes. Making money opened a whole range of opportunities for women in the Forties, both in the personal and the social aspects of their lives. Women now became active participants in the consumer culture, a fact that provoked a comfortable sense of freedom and independence. On the other hand, working in supposedly 'male jobs' proved the capacity of women to lead the country as the(ir) men were away. In sum, the War allowed them to prove they were skillful beings, capable of not only performing men's tasks, but also of keeping up with what was, up till then, considered 'women's jobs.' Women now 'wore the pants' in the family (and the country), both in the figurative and real sense, and as Eleanor Roosevelt pointed out, women turned out to be "an indispensable part of the life of the country" (qtd. in Woloch 302). The wartime industry provided a great opportunity for women who were already in the labor force and took the chance to move up into better-paid jobs and life situations. The data prove that the increase in the number of women at work during the wartime years was spectacular and "the number of married women holding jobs doubled, the age of the female labor force rose, and the number of unionized women surged from 800,000 in 1940 (9.4 percent of unionized workers) to 3 million in 1944 (21.8 percent of unionized workers)" (Woloch 302).

In these jobs, women were required to do tasks previously considered unfit for them. For this purpose, laws regarding night-time shifts and others that restricted the lifting of weights by women were temporarily changed in some states. As Woloch describes, in these new jobs, women "made airplane frames, engines, propellers, parachutes, gas masks, life rafts, artillery, munitions, and electrical equipment. They loaded shells, assembled machine guns, cleaned spark plugs, wired instrument panels, and operated hand drills, turret lathes, rivet guns, and band saws, (. . .)" (302).

The situation also favored the mobility of women, and many changed places and left their 'protective' homes to settle in new areas, new states, in a clear movement towards independence and freedom. Regardless of the fact that many women also found occupations in sectors other than the arms industry, such as in journalism, the former was much more highly paid, and many moved to the cities where this industry had boomed, including Detroit, among others. Rosie the Riveter, the image of a strong woman at work, first appeared in the *Saturday Evening Post* on May 29, 1943, and became the symbol of the woman of the Forties, who served the country and herself and took the opportunities that, sadly enough, the War brought with it. She was part of a campaign aimed at recruiting women for work and soon became the symbol of the working women of the time. Others directly joined the armed forces: "the largest number – some 140,000 – served with the Women's Army Corps (WAC), followed by 100,000 in the WAVES (Women Appointed for Volunteer Emergency Service) of the navy. A special group of women pilots made up the Women Airforce Service Pilots (WASP)" (Ware 96).

However, these opportunities for women were only temporary, as on the return of men from the War, they were pushed to return to their 'safe, feminine' homes. The clear ideological efforts that had been made during the previous decades of depression to maintain women outside the labor force were reinstated and even reinforced. Women, who were offered the opportunity, and even ordered to take it, to enter a productive, self-reliant life during the wartime years, were forced to once again come back to their protected, submitted reality. In sum, the job opportunities that arose for women (and especially for married women) during these years did not encompass a profound change in the way in which gender roles were understood in the country, but just a temporary measure, provoked by the urgency of the War, which was soon forgotten once it had ended and the men had returned to the country. Moreover, as Woloch points out, the wartime situation reinforced these hierarchical gender roles, as the situation favored the idea of male value rather than female independence. Many young women, afraid of the scarcity of men, married early, divorce rates increased because of geographical separation and working women were suspected of not being able to fulfill their female roles while working outside their homes. In this social context, after the War, strong efforts were made to keep them out of the labor force, put them 'back in their kitchens' and hire the men for work. The revival of the private sphere, the home, as a feminine space, and the idea of the domestic duties of women, were extolled again, and they saw their opportunities vanish as the country was blooming and booming after the War victory.

4.1.1. World War II and Mexican American women

In the case of Mexican American women, the demand for labor provoked by the War opened a whole new universe for these young women, too influenced and controlled by the tradition of their community, of a strong patriarchal essence. On the one hand, being able to leave the protective nest of their traditional homes and becoming part of the productive collective of the country gave them an assurance and freedom that they lacked until then. Moreover, making money and being able to administer it favored their active participation in the consumer culture of the times, and this was an essential element in the emergence of groups such as the *Pachucas*. Finally, young Mexican American women felt they were considered 'the same as the others' for the first time and their range of personal relationships increased enormously. The massive inclusion of women of all ethnic groups and classes in the factories led to the development of inter-ethnic relationships and the supposed normalization of ethnic relationships.

Among the different doors that entering the labor force, and thus having a salary, opened for women in general, and Mexican women in particular, was that of their active entrance into the leisure world. The very restrictive Mexican tradition had kept the girls protected under the umbrella of familiar or community relationships, and 'getting out from under the umbrella' and sharing time with people of other ethnic communities was a whole new discovery for Mexican girls. In the social context where the lives of citizens were determined by the War, the government made great efforts to encourage the promotion of leisure activities throughout the country, both for the anxious, desperate, scared citizens who remained on the home front and for the servicemen, who needed to be encouraged and somehow distracted from their endeavors. Thus, dances, balls and the cinema were among the most notable physical and emotional 'ways out' for the youth of the Forties.

Mexican American girls, whose socialization had always been restricted to family celebrations or community events, and had always been marked by the 'ever-present' chaperon whenever they went out, were totally thrilled by the new leisure opportunities available to them. In Vicki L. Ruiz's words, "chaperonage is best understood as a manifestation of familial oligarchy whereby elders attempted to dictate the activities of the youth for the sake of the family honor. A family's standing on the community depended, in part, on the women's purity" (51–2). For the girls, going to dances not only allowed them to dance and enjoy their free time, but it opened up a way to relate to people (and men) of their own community and to those of other ethnic groups. These new means of inter-ethnic relationships, however, encouraged the perspective of 'mixing but differentiating,' marking their own identity. The *Pachuca* style, in this sense, provided a means of reclaiming a different identity, and was thus embraced by several young girls, with the only purpose of looking cool, looking different.

But not everything was positive in the process of the liberalization of Mexican women. While they were excited about having money, spending it in their own interests and making individual choices, they were challenging both the mainstream group and their own community. The former regarded them as a racialized threat. Mexican women in general, but *Pachucas* more particularly, represented a menace to a society that needed to be united for obvious reasons. The country was at war, and every citizen had to make an effort for the country. Young Mexican American women who adopted the *Pachuco* style, however, seemed to be too worried about their own matters and appearance, and their attitude was understood as an offense to the seriousness of the War situation. On the other hand, their 'obviously loose' sexual stance, and their new capacity to relate to white men, exhibited a manifest threat to the 'stability' and purity of the white community. They shattered the norms of female propriety and decency and represented the great enemy within. As expressed by Professor Elizabeth R. Escobedo,

> To Euro-American and Mexican communities, young women deemed *Pachucas* represented a dangerous example of the increasing public role of all women during World War II. With more women entering the workforce than ever before, an anxious U.S. society feared that women with newfound freedoms would be unwilling to return to domestic life once the War ended. They might be encouraged to enter the public sphere as a wartime necessity but were simultaneously expected to maintain their femininity and sexual purity. Whether the so-called *Pachucas* actually retained "proper" sexual standards or not, their relatively short skirts, bold makeup, and more pronounced presence suggested a tainted sexual reputation, and they sounded alarms.
>
> (30)

For their parents, however, the girls were (in a way) victims of the influence of the lax sexual standards of the Anglo society, and they were just reproducing a set of behaviors they had learned when they entered the productive workforce. Moreover, these parents were also scandalized by the irreverent attitude of their daughters, who, they thought, were betraying their community and traditions. The young Mexican American women, and in particular those who adopted the *Pachuca* style, became *Malinches*, betrayers in the eyes of their group. This historical figure and posterior myth represents one of the dichotomies through which Mexican American women have always been described and 'valorized.' The good woman is represented by the *Virgen de Guadalupe*, an essentially good and virtuous woman (who accepts and transmits tradition and its encompassing gender roles). Her diametrically opposed figure, *La Malinche* (who was defined as a woman who sold her own people to the Spaniards when she married Cortés and acted as a (cultural) translator between the two communities), depicts women who follow their own path and defy tradition for the sake of their own interests, as the *Pachucas* did. In this sense, the girls' move towards freedom and agency was a twofold one, as they were concomitantly gaining a terrible reputation both inside and outside their own group, to the point of being considered betrayers themselves, and, similarly, they were compared to "amateur prostitutes" by the decent, mainstream group (Escobedo 31). The *Pachucas* became delinquents in the eyes of society and they were treated and criminalized as such.

Needless to say, not all the girls who adopted the *Pachuca* style embraced gang activity and delinquency. The majority of them just did it for fun, or as a means of reclaiming their identity and difference; others, just for fashion and style purposes. However, they were regarded and described as a homogeneous group, and thus they all unconsciously embodied highly politicized representations of contestation to the norms. Their public bodies, their exaggerated look and their obvious difference and otherness became the symbols of rebellion and, in sum, of youth and controversy. In other words,

> In fact, the persona created by *Pachucas* did take on a degree of political meaning, as the young women outwardly challenged the vision of American commonality by embracing a womanhood that emphasized cultural difference. To be sure, some Mexican American women chose to wear zoot suits for the simple reason that they liked the style or as a way to take part in peer-group socializing. Thus wearing a zoot suit was not necessarily an inherently political act but certainly few zoot-suited youth were completely oblivious to the implications of their controversial choices in appearance and behavior, particularly given the conservative context of the times.
>
> (Escobedo 359)

The *Pachuca*, in sum, became a deviant figure in the highly moralistic and patriotic Forties' sociocultural panorama, but, as will be seen in the following pages, and as has been proved by several scholars (and *Pachucas* themselves), theirs was an act of *subversion and deviation through the unconscious*.

4.2. Women's fashion in the Forties

As explained before, the new political and social situation of the country apparently and temporarily changed the male/female roles, and the entering of women into the labor force brought into question the notions of femininity and female beauty, among other issues. Many women worked in the arms industry and performed heavy physical duties, which had before been considered male ones. The image of Rosie the Riveter turned into an icon of womanhood during the wartime years, portraying the virtues of a strong woman, whose traditional physical female attributes added to some that deployed a more active, stronger woman. However, and in a parallel way, as explained by the Office of War Information (OWI), efforts were made to highlight the fact that "women have not been told in national publicity that military services do not destroy their femininity nor detract from it. There has not been sufficient emphasis on the fact that women in the Armed Forces are respected as women, and that they are not remolded into some other kind of half-male, half-female hybrid" (McEuen 43).

Before the US got involved in the War, both the garment industry and the media had reinforced the feminine standard of beauty, aligned with a very specific image of the white woman. In this sense, "the ideal manifested itself in urban America where partygoers and trendsetters bought close-fitting gowns to reveal slim outlines with long legs, narrow waists, and flat chests. Stereotypes of women of color as well as immigrant women helped promote whiteness as an ideal" (McEuen 134–5). Once the War had started, the country was immersed in a crisis that affected fashion and temporarily changed gender roles. The efforts of the garment industry to maintain its economy were obvious, and the case of the New York Dress Industry (NYDI) is an example of this. Its advertisements included: "America doesn't want its women dreary. It wants you looking nice" and "[A] woman in war must be more than the equal of a man. She must be his guiding star. Whatever war tasks she undertakes, she must still shine forth as Woman" (McEuen 137). It is interesting to highlight the way these messages exemplified the patriarchal spirit of the times. On the one hand, they clearly value the strength and capacity of women (who are defined as equal to men), and on the other they similarly struggle to maintain the very clear hegemonic patriarchal roles, where women are depicted as objects for the male gaze and desire. Such messages, however, render nonwhite women invisible, as they are presented as a standard image of the American woman, who is white and middle class. In this sense, the crossing of the private/public boundary that Mexican and other nonwhite women achieved was revolutionary *per se*, both inside and outside the realms of their communities. Coming back to the essence of the messages, despite the efforts of the garment industry to link fashion with victory, and feminine dress with patriotism, there were petitions on the part of the government that enhanced austerity and scarcity in dressing. In this regard, the War Production Board (WPB) launched restrictions such as General Limitation Order L-85, which

> [s]ought to conserve natural fibers, such as cotton, silk and wool. It also limited the domestic use of nylon and rayon. The policy demanded that dresses have narrower skirts and fewer decorative touches requiring extra fabric. A two-inch limit applied to hem depth and same fabric belts; jacket length could not exceed twenty-five inches. Balloon sleeves, turnover cuffs, double material yokes, and attached hoods and shawls were prohibited. A jacket could feature only one pocket.
>
> (McEuen 138)

Visual accounts of female fashion (such as images of institutional uniforms and the civilian style) of the times sent a clear message of austerity and decency. Even when dressed as civilians, women looked like women 'on duty.' The suits that were encouraged to be worn resembled military uniforms, with very marked lines, sober and practical. However, the restriction did not apply to wedding and maternity clothes, making clear the obvious gender-based ideology that the measure conveyed. Women were asked to work in the factories temporarily, but their inherent role in society was to get married, have kids and raise them. However, the incursion of women into the workforce brought a major significant change in the dress code of the Forties and thereafter. The work at the factories required a garment that permitted the physical work women performed: women had to wear slacks, women had to wear pants. This provoked a revolution in the personal lives of women and in the social rejection that women with pants caused. When they left their workplaces with their pants on, they were ridiculed and sometimes insulted. A difficult-to-accept change was occurring.

In the same vein, the cosmetic industry made a great effort to remain active, and manufacturers such as Pond's tried to engage women with advertising campaigns that addressed the working woman or the woman in the military forces. Thus, commercials that read "She's engaged! She's lovely! She uses Pond's" (McEuen 12) called for feminine beauty despite the restrictions of the wartime effort. The big steps towards female independence in economic and social terms that the War brought with it were, however, observed as a threat that had to be avoided, and in that sense, the efforts of the mainstream beauty industry and media in general were devoted to keeping the women "as female as possible."

4.3. The *Pachuca*: a rebel without a cause

In the above context, the 'defiant' *Pachuca* look was understood both as a provocation to the national identity and the call for utter patriotism that was key during the War, as well as to the intrinsic and natural gender roles that had maintained the cultural heritage of the nation and would be perpetuated after the War had ended. The Zoot Suit Riots were one of the means that the media found to point at the supposed anti-patriotic attitude that *Pachucas* represented. Before delving into the description of the *Pachuca* look, however, I find it interesting to shed some light onto the real participation of *Pachucas* in the riots, which would lead the way to the criminalization of these young women and their peers, and finally, of the whole Mexican American community in general.

4.3.1. Pachucas, Pachucos, *and the* Zoot Suit Riots

The Zoot Suit Riots were described by the media as originating from a fight around the discriminatory and harassing attitude of white servicemen towards the female *Pachucas*. According to Catherine Ramírez, however, the role of *Pachucas* during the riots was more relevant than described in the different accounts of the riots. These described *Pachucas* as passive and submissive women whose only role was to accompany the men, and they were thus secondary participants in the events that occurred in the year 1942. The efforts to portray the girls of Mexican origin as mere companions not only depicted them as nonexistent and silent women, but reinforced the gender roles that were predominant in the US society of the times. According to the official accounts, both the white servicemen and the *Pachucos* who were involved in the riots were the only active agents of the fights and women had no real role in them or in the events that would occur afterwards with the defense of the accused in the trials and in the face of public opinion in general. However, these women, who were criminalized but were not criminals, became very active in the public defense of their peers during the trials, as well as in the rejection of the stereotypes that were spread as a consequence of the riots.

It all started with the death of José Díaz at Sleepy Lagoon on August 1, 1942. History professor Eduardo Pagán's narration of the facts proves that José's death was a random choice. He and many of his neighbors and friends were dancing and enjoying the night in the Delgadillo family backyard, celebrating the 20th birthday of one of the Delgadillo girls. Everything was going well until some Anglo boys from Downey (a neighboring area) moaned about the lack of beers. They were then invited to leave the party. Irritated, José drove towards the Sleepy Lagoon reservoir, 'a site of love,' where lovers stayed in their cars, and friends gathered. One of the cars was occupied by Henry Leyvas and his girlfriend Dora. The Downey boys insulted them, and Henry responded. A fight broke out, many were injured and soon after the Downey group left. Henry and his friends, all dwellers on 38th Street, knew they had to react, and they drove to Sleepy Lagoon. As Obregón Pagán states,

> Clearly they could not let an assault on their peers go unpunished, but they were more likely outraged by the nature of the attack. Badly outnumbered, none of the boys stood a chance of defending themselves. (. . .) To make matters worse, in these boys' eyes, the young men who beat Leyvas also repeatedly struck Dora Baca on her arms, face, and back when she threw herself over Henry to protect him. Such an assault was an egregious violation of their fundamental sense of morality, and there was little debate or discussion about what had to be done next.
>
> (63)

Finding nobody there, some of the members of the group suggested the Downey boys might be at a party in a nearby street. Off they went, thirsty for revenge. Leyvas took one of the members of the party for the man who had attacked him and started to beat him. After a sudden attack on the participants of the family party, they left, leaving many, including the Delgadillo father, injured, and innocent José Díaz stabbed almost to death on a nearby dirt road.

The real causes of the fight and subsequent death of José Díaz are unknown, but what occurred next marked an unstoppable atmosphere of discrimination and criminalization of the Mexican American youth of the Forties. The *Los Angeles Daily News*, the *Los Angeles Examiner*, the *Los Angeles Herald* and the *Los Angeles Times*, the most influential media in the city at the time, reported that "Mexican-American zoot-suiters terrorized Los Angeles county" (Ramírez 17). However, and as many of the photographs that were published during those days show, none of the boys and girls who were accused of having participated in the Sleepy Lagoon case were wearing zoot suits, but regular shirts and trousers, and the girls, clothes that were common in the period (Ramírez 17). Following the events at the Lagoon, hundreds of Mexican American youths were arrested and finally, 23 Mexican Americans and a white boy were tried for the murder. The trial was full of inconsistencies and the all-white jury biased. They were accused of being part of an organized gang, and among other racially biased issues, Captain Edward Durán Ayes declared that Mexicans were "biologically inferior to Anglo Americans and inherently violent" because of their "Indian and Oriental (i.e. Native American) background," and "more akin to the Japanese enemy than to Americans of European descent" (Ramírez 19). The boys were furthermore not allowed to talk to their lawyers during the sessions, nor were they permitted to bathe or change clothes before the trial. The Angelino newspapers boasted about the criminal nature of Mexican youths in general, and *Pachucas* in particular, and performed a parallel, public trial of the boys and girls, strengthened by irrational feelings of racism. Only five of them were found innocent, and some of the rest were convicted to a life sentence (including Leyvas), and others to a different number of years. Ten girls were also called as witnesses to the trial. However, and according to Ramírez, the implication of the girls in the Sleepy Lagoon case and in the subsequent riots has never been accounted for in any historical review of the time. On the contrary, according to the scholar, they were not only active during the event, but also during the hearings, which they attended together with their friends, mothers and family members. Others were very actively involved in the Sleepy Lagoon Defense Committee (SLDC), and became their representatives and spokespersons. Five months after the trial and with the grounds of discrimination still alive, the Zoot Suit Riots broke out between servicemen (marines) and youths mainly in zoot suits. Many Mexican Americans were arrested and finally the Navy forbade servicemen to enter the city of Los Angeles with a view to putting an end to the riots.

In this senseless, violent context, the outfit worn by some and others (marines and zoot suiters) became essential for identifying and later beating the individuals wearing them. The zoot suit, in particular, acquired strong political connotations and was suddenly constructed as the 'other,' the defiant, nonconformist look in a time of patriotism and defense of the American values provoked by the ongoing war. The times of scarcity brought by the War had imposed a rationing not only of food and goods, but also of fabric and clothes, and new norms of propriety, decency and ultimately patriotic respect had been imposed by the situation. In fact, "by March 1942, (. . .) the War Production Board regulated the wartime manufacture of suits, creating a maximum standard for fabric to be used. In response to the continuing demand, downtown clothiers like Murray's Young's, and Earl's would sell and customize bootleg zoot suits" (Macías 72). The extravagance and expensiveness of the zoot suit was regarded as indecent by the highly patriotic servicemen, and an affront to American values. In the same vein,

> War production facilitated the introduction of working-class youths to new levels of consumption, and purchasing expensive and distinctive clothes,

acquiring a used car, or affording greater access to dances, concerts, and movies signaled their entrée into the material culture of the United States. These were not acquisitions based on middle-class notions of thrift and respectability but youthful indulgences framed by a popular culture, largely inspired by African American hipsters and jazz artists. Certainly young people were not completely aware of the scandalous reputation of jazz life or of societal expectations of thrift and sacrifice, but flaunting convention was part of what gave the music, the language, and the clothing its appeal.

The flaunting of convention came at a price, however, by feeding into public concerns about juvenile delinquency. The more that drape shapes were seen on the streets of Los Angeles – (. . .) – the more that zoot-suited "menace" appeared to be a growing problem.

(Obregón Pagán 120)

Moreover, the suit soon became a symbol of a 'marked ethnicity,' as it was mainly worn by African American and Mexican American youths. This reinforced the idea of betrayal of a country that needed the support of all its members, and carried with it a direct criminalization of those wearing it. The zoot suiters became the targets of the 'very loyal' marines, and tearing apart their outfit, and stripping them of their clothes, was one of the main aims of the servicemen, who thought leaving the boys naked, without their mark of identity, was their best punishment. Boys and girls entered the American consumption scheme and formed part of the social system, a system that at the same time expelled them.

The zoot suit, thus, became a sign of a time and a community, but was soon turned into a criminal, delinquent, indecent, unpatriotic one, and was thus subject to being fought against and eradicated. In this context, removing the *Pachucos'* clothes, become, for the servicemen, a proof of patriotism (and of *macho* bravery). According to Kate Soper,

> to take a person's clothing is to put him or her "out on the heath," to snatch away the clutched straw of human dignity. As all prison camp guards and torturers have been well aware, to force strip the victim is to initiate the process of dehumanization, to signal contempt for personal identity by playing with or mocking at the aspiration to preserve it. The power of denuding the other in these contexts is also the power to depersonalize the other's clothing or adornment.
>
> (21)

Leaving the boys naked, unsuited in the street, thus implied, on the one hand, the elimination of all traces of group identification. Once the *Pachuco* was naked and his suit destroyed, he was deprived of this most evident marker of identity and belonging, which was his suit. Moreover, the fact that the servicemen destroyed the young *Pachucos'* suit implied the erasure of their means of social rebellion. The suit, which acquired a strong signification of youthful rebellion, as well as of ethnic identification, was wrecked, and the young *Pachucos* were left naked, desocialized and thus, animalized and otherized in front of the general public. On the other hand, the marine's uniform, scrupulously clean and white, represented a commitment to a country that needed all its members' effort. In this context, the meaning of the two outfits was soon filled with signification and the criminalization of the *Pachuco* and *Pachuca* was very easily carried out. The communicative role of both outfits, as revealed by Barnard (2002), gave way to the essentialization and hierarchization of both groups, which were very soon put in an unbalanced position of power, where some were considered national heroes and the others betrayers of the country. What is clear, however, is that zoot suiters (both men and women) were rebellious young kids, who expressed their uneasiness towards a society (both the Mexican American and the mainstream society) they considered did not believe in them fully because of the way they dressed, which marked them as belonging to a specific, nonstandard and thus deviant group. As expressed by Marilyn Horn, they sought group cohesiveness and thus fought what she calls "the external threats to their existence":

> Every individual needs the security and distinction of knowing that he belongs to a particular group within the mass society. The extent to which he identifies with any group or class depends upon his own consciousness or awareness of the group's existence as well as knowledge of his own relative status or position. People are more strongly motivated to conform to the standards of the group to which they feel they should belong, rather than the group or class to which they might be assigned on the basis of external criteria.
>
> Feelings of group belongingness are greatly enhanced by (1) giving its constituents an emblem of membership, (2) giving it a name, and (3) external threats to its existence. Clothing is probably the most conspicuous and the most visual of all possible badges of group belongingness. Criticism of group standards of dress tends to increase group cohesiveness and the compulsion to conform to the established norms.
>
> (170)

This same cohesiveness, however, marked them as easily identifiable characters, looked upon as a unitary group, and their criminalization process was easily carried out, and supported by the dominant majority. Similarly, and as part of the group, the women who dared not only stand up in the streets but also defy the rules of decency, morality and feminine patriotism were very rapidly 'otherized' and criminalized. Their obvious divergent appearance, furthermore, facilitated this discriminatory move towards these women, who were soon turned into deviant others, suspected of being, and described as, the representation of evil and deviation, regardless of their individual realities. Because when they "exhibited their expressive culture in the public sphere, more reactionary elements in the city sought to exoticize them and criminalize them in order to minimize their importance" (Macías 91). Finally, "these Mexican American women, both *Pachucas* and squares, protested accusations of deviance and immorality by defending their virginity and respectability" (Macías 90).

The media, on the other hand, supported said categorization of *Pachucos/as* (and marines), who were always presented as two opposing forces, the former representing evil and the latter goodness and patriotism. As an example, two pieces of news which were placed contiguously in the *Los Angeles Times* of June 10, 1943, show a group of forming naval candidates on the left side of the page, and just to its right, a photograph of two *Pachucos*. The image of the naval candidates represents purity, order and control, while contrasting with that is the photograph of Luis Verdusco, alias "The Chief," who was "arraigned yesterday on charge of violating the deadly weapons act in zoot suit arrests." Moreover, a photograph on his right of Frank Tellez, modeling "a zoot suit in County jail. Tellez says he holds medical discharge from the Army," clearly establishes a direct link between the zoot suit and its violent, deadly and unpatriotic meaning and implications.

4.3.2. The Pachuca style politics

Regardless of the fact that the Forties and the World War II period represented a step forward in the process of the acquisition of freedom and visibility for young Mexican women, the *Pachuca* is still inevitably related to the *Pachuco* male figure. This and his zoot suit became symbols of some kind of 'rebellion' against the established status quo, both represented by the mainstream society and the Mexican American community. Theirs, however, was a subconscious rebellion that brought the uttermost affront to the American national discourse of the War and post-War United States and created a strong sense of moral panic (Cohen 2002 (1972)), which could only be eradicated by a fierce attack on the part of the mainstream moral apparatus.

Mexican young girls, for their part, also adopted this rebellious attitude, and their physical appearance, amongst other issues, became the voice of their defiance towards everything that had previously been settled. Even if the *Pachuca* look was not as clearly defined as the male zoot suit, in general terms, *Pachucas* wore short skirts (above the knees generally), a very exaggerated hairstyle and abundant makeup. All in all, *Pachucas* sought to be different and break the norms through their attire and look. Catherine S. Ramírez describes the general look adopted by both *Pachucas* and *Pachucos* like this:

> For young Mexican American women in wartime Los Angeles, the zoot look generally consisted of a cardigan or V-neck sweater and a long, broad-shouldered "finger-tip" coat; a knee-length and therefore relatively short pleated skirt; fishnet stockings or bobby socks; and platform heels, saddle shoes, or huarache sandals. Many also wore dark lipstick and used foam inserts called "rats" to lift their hair into a high bouffant. For extra panache, some lightened their hair with peroxide, sported tattoos, or wore the masculine version of the zoot suit. Also known as "drapes" or el tacuche, this outfit

consisted of the "finger-tip" coat, which sometimes extended to the knee, a pair of billowing "Punjab" pants that tapered at the ankle. Some Mexican American male zooters added a long watch chain and hat (called a tando) to the ensemble, but many abandoned their relatively long hair into a pompadour on top and what was known as an "Argentine ducktail" or "duck's ass" ("D.A.") in back. Calcos or thick-soled shoes often punctuated the look.

(xii)

No doubt about it, the *Pachuca/o* look was an elaborate one, and despite its conscious (or not) political implications, it aimed at grabbing people's attention. So, what was the symbolic meaning of the *Pachuca* style? Were these young girls defying the norms, did their attire convey some kind of protest or was it just 'fashion'?

A direct relationship between those girls (and boys) wearing the *Pachuco* outfit and the supposedly 'criminal' activities of the *Pachuco* gangs is hard to prove. Some of the youths who identified themselves with others by means of their attire did not consider themselves *Pachucas*, and they were not part of any organized, criminal group. The *Pachuco/a* outfit was one of voluntary contestation, but became a matter of discrimination and prejudice, especially during the violent Zoot Suit Riots in the year 1942 in Los Angeles. The origins of the riots were presented in many mainstream media as arising from the need of *Pachucos* to control their women, who were considered loose and sexually active by the marines. The media of the time played an important part in portraying the *Pachuca* as a physically excessive, dark, provocative, and dangerous woman. A piece of news (and its accompanying photographs) from the *Washington Daily News* of June 11, 1943, with the heading *Zoot Suiters Run for Cover but Their "Cholitas" Carry On*, is a clear example of the double standard with which these women were described and represented: on the one hand, as aggressively active women, and on the other, as servile companions to their male peers, as their *Cholitas*. The beginning of the news marks a clear racially discriminating description of the *Pachuca* as a racially marked individual:

> Dark-eyed "cholitas" packing razors in the tops of their black mesh stockings today took up the street fighting where their male zoot-suit counterparts were forced to drop it. Garbed entirely in midnight black, with an above-the-knee version of the hobble skirt, they grandiosely vowed to carry the battle against servicemen and police "until one side or the other is wiped out."
>
> Three of them attacked a waitress coming out of a downtown tunnel, knocked her down and slashed her with a razor.

The description of the *Pachucas*' attire, demeanor and actions is reinforced by the two opposing photographs that the news presents. The girls are first presented in a condescending way by means of the utilization of the diminutive form *Cholitas* instead of *Cholas*. Similarly, the use of the possessive pronoun 'their,' making reference to the lack of agency on the part of these women, reinforces the idea of the gender submission of Mexican American women. This idea, however, is counteracted by the clearly aggressive act of wiping either the police or the servicemen out and the fact that they are described as carrying deadly weapons, which they use randomly, as proved by the stabbing of the innocent waitress, who is portrayed as naïve and scared. Moreover, the description of the young girls also reflects a certain moral position on the part of the journalist, who describes the fact that they are dressed in midnight black (implying their being out on the streets at times when proper, decent women should not be), and finally makes an extraordinary comment on the above-the-knee skirt, which is obviously presented as an affront to the standards of decency of proper females.

News like the above-mentioned encouraged the criminalization of the *Pachuca*, which was parallel to that of their male counterparts. They were represented as disloyal to the country, aggressive, criminal, and delinquent women, and on top of everything else, as sexually active and 'whore-like.' Similarly, other media of the time, in a very contradictory way, portrayed the *Pachuca* as a woman who remained passive during the riots, as her only role was that of the companion who had to be saved from the gender aggressions of the white servicemen (Ramírez). In Ramírez's words, the press favored a "discourse that positions Mexican and Mexican American women as simple pawns in a conflict between discrete groups of men [that] renders them passive, interchangeable objects, rather than active historical agents" (41). These Mexican girls and their 'indecent' attitude challenged the norms not only of patriotic commitment and propriety, but also those of female behavior and decorum. The girls who opted for wearing a look similar to that of their male counterparts became, in the eyes of the mainstream community and often their own community, loose, lewd women, but who were still always presented as submissive and passive, in a highly contradictory way.

However, in her study of the meaning of the *Pachuca* style in general and the degree of identification of these girls with the supposedly organized, criminal gang of *Pachucas*, Catherine S. Ramírez proves that most of the girls who adopted the *Pachuca* style did not see themselves as *Pachucas*, or part of any particular gang. In fact, the author posits that the *Pachuca* has been excluded from any historical and sociological study, and even from the foundational discourse of *Chicano* nationalism. She describes these women as invisible to the eyes of their contemporary peers, as well as the forthcoming generations. However, the *Pachuca* is, for the scholar, an incredibly rich source of information when trying to understand the formation of a *Chicano* nationalist identity. She represents a source of contestation and struggle in terms of gender and sexual vindication. Hence, it is one of my aims to defend that the *Pachuca*, regardless of her deliberate or non-deliberate attitude and position, is and was a political figure, and her rebellious stance became essential for the development of the subsequent and more politically elaborate *Chicana* feminist identity and thought. The *Pachuca* represented deviance, challenge and, ultimately, agency, and thus she was highly political and hers was a step towards *subversion and deviation through the conscious*.

The *Pachuca*, with her short skirt and elaborate hairstyle, accompanying the *Pachuco*, became a threat, in the eyes of both her parents and the mainstream society. The former panicked at the thought that their daughter was not Mexican enough, was leaving their tradition and was becoming 'too American.' The mainstream society, represented by the mass media (amongst other institutions and individuals), regarded her as un-American, unpatriotic and immoral. The *Pachuca* embodied, with her look and attitude, both negative marks of ethnicity and sexuality, and she became, once again, decidedly political. Her knees – her brown knees, audaciously for some, provocatively for others – were a mark of defiance and agency, and represented a daring step towards the acquisition of visibility, both inside and outside their group. In this sense, the *Pachuca* became "dangerously masculine, monstrously feminine" (Ramírez 20).

However, and despite the efforts of the media to criminalize both *Pachucos* and *Pachucas*, many of them lived a 'regular' existence, void of criminality and unlawful actions. For many *Pachucas*, in fact, their outfit did represent some degree of rebellion against the established norms, but in most cases, they were far from the postulates of gangs and illegal activities. According to Escobedo,

> Those Mexican American women who were typically thought to be "*Pachuca*" – regardless of whether or not they self-identified as such – blatantly rebelled against Mexican and mainstream American social conventions by donning a zoot suit or a modified version of the male attire, a look that varied but often included a fingertip coat, a relatively short skirt, dark lipstick and pompadoured hair. (. . .) But more than just a fashion rebel, the so-called *Pachuca* flaunted a sense of self that played with sexuality and highlighted cultural differences, posing a direct challenge to both second-class citizenship in the United States and rigid, static notions of Mexican femininity. Although numerous Mexican American women worked, volunteered, and wore the zoot look during the War, the Mexican community and the larger populace focused on the latter behavior, condemning their particular style of rebellion.
>
> (9–10)

In sum, and regardless of the fact that many of them did not consciously identify with *la Pachucada*, these girls became highly political beings, and their attitude and look turned into a defiant challenge to everything that had until then defined their existence. The *Pachuca* broke the norms of aesthetic behavior, she entered actively into the consumption culture, she reinterpreted the role and attitude of the traditional Mexican woman, making herself visible and, finally, she became a sexually visible different, racial woman, eager to be seen and taken into account. What for many was just an act of fashion, style and look became the beginnings of an unstoppable political act, whose implications were to be seen some decades afterwards. The *Pachuca* was/is political and her look and style was/is political too. The *Pachuca* was a woman, a different woman, calling for discernibility and agency. In Professor Escobedo's words, "more than just a fashion rebel, the Wartime *Pachuca* represented an important symbolic site on which debates regarding the changing social landscape of the War years unfolded" (18).

Regardless of the fact that there are only a few public representations of *Pachucas* of the Forties which are not related to the Zoot Suit Riots, some of the photographs taken during the Zoot Suit era (some of which have been collected in Ramírez's volume on *Pachucas* and others in diverse digital sources) are examples of the description of the *Pachuca* as a symbolic site, as expressed by Escobedo.

This image in Figure 4.1, entitled *La Pachuca*, conceived as a representation of la *Pachuca* of the Forties, may well serve me as a starting point. The woman in the photograph, who is posing for it presents all the external-look traits that have been described so far. She is wearing a female version of the characteristic *Pachuca* zoot suit, regardless of the fact that her pants are not as baggy as those worn by her male counterparts. Her long jacket or drape provides her with a masculine look, which is 'balanced' by her elaborate hairstyle, which consists of a high pompadour. The black-and-white image allows the viewer to infer that she has red lips, and in sum, she is the essential representation of the *Pachuca*. However, and relating this description and the photograph itself to the previously mentioned objectification and criminalization of the *Pachuca* by the Angelino press, especially during the Zoot Suit Riots, the attitude and facial expression of the woman in the photograph give out no message of aggressiveness or defiance, as will be observed in those of the end-of-the-century *Cholas*. The obvious *subversion and deviation through the conscious* that the acquisition of a male attire symbolized during the Forties, aimed at challenging both the general public and the traditional Mexican American community, is, however, not reinforced by the young woman's body language, which is far from being rebellious or aggressive.

Similarly, Figure 4.2 presents the image of a young Mexican American woman posing in front of a camera. As with the previous one, two main conclusions can be arrived at when looking at the picture. On the one hand, the attitude of the woman is one of pride and self-consciousness, but it is never a defiant, criminal one, as many of these young men and women were portrayed in the media, especially during the Zoot Suit Riots.

The photograph, in contrast to the previous one, is taken in a more natural setting, and regardless of the fact that the woman is posing for it, the general atmosphere that is represented in it is one of quotidianity and naturalness. A first glance at the image from a 21st century perspective, however, would make one infer that the woman's look, unusual and probably shocking for the time, had a less rebellious feeling to it than that of the previous *Pachuca*. Her hairstyle is obviously elaborate and consists of a high pompadour, and so are her prominent earrings, which, together with the hairdo, provide the woman with a sophisticated and obviously deviant image compared to the one that was standard for women at the time. Moreover, her big jacket, which could be considered a female version of the male zoot jacket or drape, also hints at a different rebellious look that obviously conveyed a message of nonconformity at that time. But very probably, it was her above-the-knee short skirt that

Figure 4.1 Portrait of Ramona
Courtesy of LA Public Library. Shades of LA Collection

Figure 4.2 Woman wearing a zoot suit
Courtesy of LA Public Library. Shades of LA Collection

made the woman's look nonstandard and very probably irreverent for the times. This leads to the second obvious conclusion that looking at the woman's image, her look, posture and overall attitude takes us to: the fact that her look was *consciously* elaborated to very probably *unconsciously express subversion and deviation*. The woman's attitude, which, as can be seen in her facial and bodily expression, is far from being aggressive or challenging, but was received by the mainstream community as such, aggressive and challenging, and it was finally criminalized by the press. However, conscious as the woman was of her own personal image, her and her peers' main objective was far from expressing anger, but rather a juvenile disconformity towards the status quo, both in their community and in the mainstream one, and a sense of ingenuous rebellion that led to a fierce criminalization of their image, their selves and bodies, and finally their whole community, that of Mexican Americans. This fact was used for the purpose of control, which is generally exerted by the dominant groups that respond to the "official concern over delinquency" (Griffin 101), which is supported by discourses that assume the "presumed superiority of Anglo-European middle-class cultures" and are "reinforced through repeated comparisons with the numerous supposedly negative dimensions of 'Other' cultural forms" (Griffin 101).

The essentialization and general banning of the *Pachuca* community from the mainstream discourse was, however, directly related to issues of ethnic and racial hierarchization of the North American society of the Forties. The social situation that the War had immersed the country in, where most males were at war and the gender and social arrangement of the country had been deeply affected, was cleverly utilized by the media (and in particular, by the Los Angeles newspapers) to point at the whole Mexican community, which was abundant in the southwest of the country. In this sense, the riots that occurred in the year 1942 in Los Angeles were but an excuse to favor an intricate move towards the ethnic division of the city in particular, California and finally the country, which justified the public demonization of people of Mexican descent. The women who had adopted the *Pachuca* look, like those in Figure 4.3, were obviously women who expressed rebellion and disconformity against the norm. Their masculine attire, the baggy pants and their 'nonusual' hairstyles were, for many, an attention-seeking call that had to/could be punished.

Very probably, however, what offended the mainstream society, evilly influenced by the Angelino media, was not these women's attire and different (deviant) look, but their brownness and nonwhite (and thus nonstandard) bodies and their shameless, proud, public exhibition. The Zoot Suit Riots were thus utilized as a means of ethnic hierarchization and categorization of a group, for purposes other than decency and/or morality. There are, however, other visual accounts that show that their brownness was not a norm, and the feature that really showed them as a group was their different look and attitude, which, once again, was far from being defiant, challenging or dangerous.

Pachucas, women whose role was clearly defined by both their group, which wanted them inside the walls of their homes and fulfilling the roles of mothers and

Figure 4.3 Women outside San Fernando Studio
Courtesy of LA Public Library. Shades of LA Collection

wives, and an Anglo-dominated social arrangement, which wanted them invisible and controlled in their *barrios*, were out in the streets, and that defiant move made them dangerous.

The joy of experiencing life outside the control of family and social structures was, finally, the menace that *Pachucas* represented, a threat to a patriarchal norm, which was, eventually, present in both the Mexican and Anglo communities. Some of the few photographs that have been made public and which represent *Pachucas* portray groups of independent, self-conscious women whose attire challenges the norm, and who finally embody happiness, empowerment and a self-chosen identity. Some of them, dressed in pants, redefine the male *Pachuco* look and make it their own, in a move that symbolizes the agency of women to reinterpret the roles and find a space on their own for their lives and vindications. Similarly, the group of three girls in Figure 4.3, whose deviance arises mostly from their elaborate, exaggerated hairstyles and their short, 'indecent' skirts, show determination and free will, and they are the symbol of the fact that women want to have a space of their own outside the protected and constrained space that the family house, with its patriarchal norms, represents. This move, a precursor of the revolution to come that would occur in the Sixties, however, was considered an affront, and these women's *subversion and deviation through the unconscious* was targeted fiercely and used to create an enormous moral and hierarchical gap between the white, dominating society and the others – in this particular case, Mexicans.

In this context, as previously explained, the Zoot Suit Riots marked a turning point in Anglo and Mexican relationships and drew attention to the latter as criminals and unpatriotic, as opposed to the dutiful white marines, who were serving the country, while the lazy Mexicans spent their money on their exaggerated outfits. Similarly, the *Pachucas* were regarded as immoral women who avoided their patriotic duty and spent the time they should be taking care of their families while the men were away at war out in the streets, as loose, unprudish women. The domino effect of criminalization and subsequent victimization of the Mexican American youth of the Forties and Fifties was effective and productive, and the efforts to present all Mexicans as one single, unitary community provoked the desired effect. In the case of the *Pachuca*, she was always described after the riots as being in the shadow of the male *Pachucos*, targets of all anger and public lynching. The young girls, who were seeking their empowerment and personal choice through their bodily revolution, however, were always presented as one to the male *Pachucos* and considered mere companions of the boys. Some of the pictures, however, show that these young people, when in groups, created a clear sense of homogeneity and belonging, but it is my view that the girls in them were self-conscious ones who dared defy the established norms of physical appearance and its consequences in terms of social attitude and position.

Other images of the moment show that it was the girls who were really deviant in terms of the fashion of the times, and the men's attire and look, extravagant as they may have appeared to many, presented no clear hint of an ostensible deviation from the norms. In some photographs, the women show that their excessive hairstyles, their wide pants and masculine coats, or their very short skirts, presented them in the public eye as rebellious women, who contested all norms of propriety with their look and style. Their very conscious choice in terms of their external appearance may well be regarded, in this context, as a political, ideological act, full of meaning and signification. Their style, which could be considered 'anti-fashion,' was very probably

> viewed as a means of making a message about the group that embraces it. It often reflects beliefs, attitudes and ideas of subcultures of the larger culture. The dress functions as a sign of rejection of the norm and hence the status quo, as well as an adherence to thought and ideas of the fringe of society. Anti-fashion can be rebellious in nature and make a statement through its style that clearly says no to the hegemony of the prevailing style of fashion.
> (Cunningham and Voso Lab 14)

In this particular case, their rebellion (fully conscious or not) was not only aimed at dressing and fashion styles, but at the expression of gender, ethnic and class norms and expectations through clothing and attitudinal codes. Their nonelaborated political discourse and agenda, on the other hand, was, in my view, the most 'aggressive' and direct affront and act of rebellion towards the mainstream status quo and their community's patriarchal and constraining norm. The *Pachucas'* unconscious act of subversion represents the most powerful one in terms of the three female communities that are the focus of this study. The *Pachucas* dressed to exist, dressed to resist and received, as a result, the most aggressive movement of defense by the mainstream power apparatus.

When the riots occurred, the *Pachucas*, like the *Pachucos*, were objectified and described as an essential group with the sole purpose of criminalizing them as a stable community. The photographs that appeared in the Los Angeles press after some *Pachucas* were detained showed them as a unitary group. In them, they were deprived of all hints of individuality and personal identity. They are all wearing short skirts except for one of the women who is wearing pants. However, the attire that they chose gave them independence, autonomy and a sense of choice, marked them as offenders and they were persecuted as belonging to a criminal organization just because of their external identification as *Pachucas*. The strong attack on the part of the Los Angeles press on *Pachucos* in particular, and people of Mexican origin in general, gave way to an arbitrary persecution of a people in the name of patriotism and the defense of American values.

The *Pachuca* look (as well as that of the *Pachuco*), in sum, acquired an even stronger weight of signification. For these women, it implied a step towards their agency and freedom. For the mainstream press and public, instead, it implied a national offense that had to be punished and persecuted. Undoubtedly, the *Pachucas' subversion and deviation through the unconscious*, or their personal small rebellion against the destiny decided for them by both their community and that of the mainstream, became the seed of what would be described as the *Chicana* feminist movement in the coming decades. The *Pachucas'* naïve defiance thus became not only a personal but also a political affront that inspired the revolution to come.

Chapter 5

Chicanas

Fighting the norm in the Seventies

5.1. Life and expectations for US women in the Seventies

The economic stability and growth in the aftermath of World War II, together with the return of men into the workforce, brought women back to the domestic sphere. The expansion of the suburban areas, which provoked the marked division of roles and spaces within families, took women back to their homes and far from public life. Women who had been out in the streets and out in the factories during World War II, women who had experienced what it meant to have a job of their own, money of their own and, in sum, a life of their own, were pushed back to the most traditional roles of child-bearers, home carers and male companions. According to historian Nancy Woloch, "the 1950s were a decade of early marriages and young families. After the War, the average marriage age for women dropped to twenty. By 1951, one woman in three was married by nineteen, and in 1958, more women married between fifteen and nineteen than in any comparable age span" (320). In this new context, women were required to be socially and personally passive, and the domestic realm favored this quiet and calm that was suddenly demanded from the previously agentic, almost independent women during the War years.

The domestic ideology that prevailed in this era, however, was soon brought into question by individual women who felt they had a "problem that has no name" (Friedan), as well as by women who began to name this so-called problem. One such voice that became essential for the growth of the forthcoming feminist movement was that of Betty Friedan, who, with her groundbreaking work *The Feminine Mystique* (1963), planted the seeds for the female rebellion that was to come in the ensuing decades. A journalist herself, Friedan anticipated a revolution and similarly took the 'feminine cause' into public opinion, and thus turned it into a political issue. Her work denounced the fact that women had returned to their homes after the War, and described women's lives in the following way:

> Millions of women lived their lives in the image of those pretty pictures of the American suburban housewife, kissing their husbands goodbye in front of the picture window, depositing their stationwagonsful of children at school,

and smiling as they ran the new electric waxer over the spotless kitchen floor. They baked their own bread, sewed their own and their children's clothes, kept their new washing machines and dryers running all day. They changed the sheets on the beds twice a week instead of once, took the rug-hooking class in adult education, and pitied their poor frustrated mothers, who had dreamed of having a career. Their only dream was to be perfect wives and mothers; their highest ambition to have five children and a beautiful house, their only fight to get and keep their husbands. They had no thought for the unfeminine problems of the world outside the home; they wanted the men to make the major decisions. They gloried in their roles as women, and wrote proudly on the census blank: "Occupation: housewife."

(18)

This apparent happy life, however, caused great dissatisfaction among women, who had found the only fulfillment of their femininity through the completion of the above-mentioned duties. Women had a problem, according to Friedan, which originated from the fact that "our culture does not permit women to accept or gratify their basic needs as human beings, a need which is not solely defined by their sexual role" (77). Friedan's work, relevant as it was for the emergence of a feminist ideology in the ensuing years, was controversial and divided women's attitude towards 'the problem.' The journalist received all kinds of responses as an answer to her work, and many were the women who defended their role and clearly stated their right and choice to maintain it as such, perpetuating the gender roles it clearly defined.

Among those women who claimed an active role outside the realm of the domestic sphere were women workers who had either kept working after the War ended or those who sought a job outside their homes. This, however, did not keep them from having children and being mothers and wives, and by the Sixties, 30 percent of mothers worked (also) outside their homes (Woloch 328). For many, these women became careless, noncommitted mothers. For many others, they were women who not only performed their 'homely duties' but also became active in the decision-making moments in their homes, and contributed to educating their kids towards self-esteem and respect, regardless of their sex, and "grew up with the expectation that women, as well as men, would play active roles in the outside world" (Chafe 392). However, the labor situation of these women was far from being ideal, as their wages differed greatly from those of their male counterparts, a situation that was brought to an end with the passing of the Equal Pay Act in 1963, which guaranteed equal salaries for the same jobs for men and women. Moreover, and in this changing atmosphere, the incursion of women into college education began to be a fact that marked the spirit of the decade, and by the Sixties, 35 percent of women had achieved a college degree (Woloch 334). In this moving context, and according to Nancy Woloch, "the Sixties provided an enlarged supply of educated women, the prime movers in the new feminism; a liberated social climate, with a growing emphasis on personal fulfillment; and finally, a new political climate, characterized by protest, activism, and militancy" (333).

One of the several activist militant groups that emerged from this sociopolitical context was NOW (National Organization of Women), and Betty Friedan herself was a prominent member of it. Among its many goals was the passing of an amendment to Title VII of the Civil Rights Act of 1964, which not only ensured the prohibition of discrimination in employment on the basis of race, but also on sex. Among the claims of NOW, we should highlight the following one, which was "to take action to bring women into full participation in the mainstream of American society now, exercising all the privileges and responsibilities thereof in truly equal partnership with men" (now.org). These women were soon brought into question by younger, more radical emerging feminists, who were grounded on the ideology of the New Left and organized in student groups such as the SDS (Students for a Democratic Society) and SNCC (Student Nonviolent Coordinating Committee), and who regarded Friedan and her followers as middle-class bourgeoisie, and demanded a thorough and effective consciousness raising among the women and the members of the diverse civil rights movements, which promoted sexual inequality while defending and claiming civil rights for all. For them, sexism was at the root of the discrimination against women, and

> sexism was institutionalized in the family and in government, in the schools and in law. It pervaded religion, the economy, and social life. It assigned to men and women different character traits, personalities, and social roles, which were methodically instilled from infancy. Sexism ensured that men would be the primary, most valuable members of society, and that women would assume a secondary, subordinate place. (. . .) The elimination of sexism, like the elimination of racism, therefore called for a drastic transformation. It meant changing values and attitudes, behavior and institutions. Getting rid of sexism, according to the ideology of women's liberation, meant both a massive awakening and fundamental social change or "revolution."
> (Woloch 346)

The clash between the two wage demands of feminists was obvious, as NOW members thought the radical feminists were pushing their demands too far, as theirs was a utopian demand, while the younger group of women considered the former too mild and institutionalist, and their demands superficial and not sufficient to attack the overall impact and negative effect of sexism in society and its functioning as a whole.

In this turbulent, yet of change and process/progress context, also grew the *Chicana* feminist movement, which was key to the changing of the situation of the *Chicana* woman both in her personal and public domains and realities. If Friedan claimed for equal treatment and rights in the public sphere and the more radical feminists defended the need to break with sexism from the basis of the social arrangement, women of color in the United States claimed a more profound revision of the social structure of the nation, which for them was not only grounded on a sexist basis but also on an extremely discriminatory race and class hierarchization of society. This, added to the inert sexism that the young feminists denounced, was the triple origin of their relegation to the lowest position in society, as well as of their personal disenfranchisement and status of social neglect and exclusion. In this situation of silence and repression, the *Chicana* feminist movement did not get organized until almost a decade later (the 1969 *Chicano Youth Liberation Conference* was in fact "one of the main events that sparked the *Chicana* movement" (*What Is the Chicana Movement?*)). Its claims not only called for the revision of the mainstream binary gender-based organization of the social arrangement in general, and social institutions in particular, but also demanded a profound questioning of the cultural and historical legacy upon which their own collective cultural *ethos* was grounded. The *Chicana* feminists, who aimed to join the *Movimiento Chicano*, which was mainly led by male activists, found fierce opposition from their male peers and miscomprehension and a lack of empathy from the white feminists. The former, the *Movimiento* men, soon identified the women's plight as a direct affront to the community's values, and considered the women *Malinches*, betrayers. Under the idea that "you make the coffee, we make the speeches" (Martínez, qtd. in Bebout 107), the *Chicano* activists sought auxiliary help from their female peers, and rejected any kind of agency and demand, which they deemed unnecessary. Similarly to what had occurred with the emergence of LULAC (League of United Latin American Citizens) or the UFW (United Farm Workers), where two models of female participation had occurred, those of "Dolores Huerta, whose style of leadership fit a 'male' model of labor organizing, with the more common but not less vital endeavors of women such as Helen Chávez, whose activism fit a more 'female' model of collective action – that is, work performed often behind the scenes, in an auxiliary or supportive fashion. (. . .)" (Flores 202), *Chicano* men demanded an auxiliary collaboration from their female peers. The clash with the white feminists that were struggling powerfully during those years was also a turning point in the articulation of a *Chicana* feminist movement, which accounted for all the demands that the socioethnic, economic, and cultural situation of these women required. These, committed to demanding equal rights and demolishing sexism, did not find it essential to include a wider theorization of women's oppression on the grounds of race and class, as they understood sexism only to be at the root of discrimination against any woman of any condition at any situation and in any place. In this unfavorable context, the *Chicana* feminists sought to define and develop a group-specific set of demands and direct actions, which started from reclaiming a revision of the culturally essential icons that most subjected the Mexican and *Chicana* woman, such as *La Virgen de Guadalupe*, *La Malinche* and *La Llorona*, among others. For this purpose, the first *Chicana* feminists had to find ways to raise their voice, break the stereotypes and reach their group and society as a whole, making themselves visible and voiced. Feminist theory and literary practice became two of the most valid tools for breaking the boundaries and chains that had kept the *Chicanas* trapped in the domestic realm and silent within the nationalist cultural imagination of the group. Moreover, and in a more practical stance, the *Chicana* feminists sought and fought for control over their body and sexuality, a fact that materialized in the breaking of the traditional codes of behavior and conduct established by the group. The body and its control became, therefore, the most personal tool for the *Chicana* empowerment and, as a consequence, the way a woman should look, dress and act became political tools that were now in the hands of every individual woman. The body became political, the body became a text that conveyed meaning and political defiance. The *Chicana* dressed to express, the *Chicana* acted to reclaim a voice.

5.2. Women's fashion in the Sixties

The Sixties were, undoubtedly, a time of revolution, evolution and change, which also affected the physical and attitudinal customs and needs of society, and particularly of women. The forthcoming hippie revolution, the civil rights movement and particularly the feminist movement gave rise to a new way of understanding social relationships, individuality, gender, social expectations and, among many other issues, fashion and external social appearance. In Jonathan Walford's words, in fact, "the Sixties saw the death of fashion and the rise of style" (7). However, there was still a powerful *haute couture* industry, and Paris had to learn to share protagonism and markets with the Italian and New York industries. However, the real revolution in terms of clothing habits and in the understanding of clothing and personal style as a system of communication came from the emergence of a young community, or of young people as a social group with consuming capabilities. The young people in different countries, eager to disassociate themselves from the previous generations, created street styles of their own, which the big fashion companies had to follow and reinterpret. Thus, the rockers, mods, yé-yés and finally the hippies appropriated the production of a personal and communal style, in what would therefore be looked at as 'youth culture.' The miniskirt, popularized by Chanel and the model Twiggy, created a sense of moral panic (Cohen 2002 (1972)) for many and offered a real sense of liberation for the women who proudly wore it. In Ruth Rubinstein's words, "in the Sixties the feminine fashion ideal was represented by Twiggy and Jean Shrimpton, two models who were exceptionally slender and wore short, childlike dresses that left large expanses of body exposed" (211).

Similarly, the mid-Sixties were influenced by fresh moves towards the liberation of the female body, and designers and street girls opted to adopt clothing that exposed the female body in, for many, scandalous ways. But regardless of the street and design tendencies that were followed during the Sixties, the "doing your own thing" or "the rise of nonconformism" (Walford 127) characterized this period with regards to the public exposure of the individual's body and self. The quest for vintage clothing and the individualization of it was a trend and "in the US vintage was transformed by the hippie movement into more of an expression of rebellion against conformity and affluence. The wearing of Victorian scarlet military tunics carried no political message in the UK, but in the US a khaki army surplus jacket worn with a flower in a buttonhole silently protested against the war in Vietnam" (Walford 131). The hippie counterculture and its style thus became a political statement *per se*, which brought great controversy with it. For instance,

> [h]ippie women wore long hair, a fact that did not upset elders. They also tied hair back in ponytails and used bandanas to keep hair out of the eyes. Beads around the neck accompanied by lockets did not surprise. Low-cut blouses, however, drew disapproval, especially when it was obvious that many female hippies did not wear bras. (. . .) Blouses sometimes left the midriff bare, and the belly button could be decorated. Hippie women also wore male work shirts, which were less suggestive than low-cut blouses, but raised questions about a proper devotion to femininity. (. . .) Many hippie women followed the beatniks by refusing to use makeup, which was a startling break with social customs. The natural look was a philosophical position that affirmed authenticity, but also saved money. (. . .) Hippie women's jewelry was often homemade. Native American beads or other exotic pieces from non-Western nations were worn.
>
> (Rorabaugh 104–5)

The hippie revolution gave women the chance to seek and fight for their own destinies and they connected with the feminist movement, which also influenced the fashion of the Seventies. This was embodied in models such as Lauren Hutton, "who personified the natural look and the image of the modern women; energetic and engaged in purposeful action and able to play many roles" (Rubinstein 212). The female roles and models that embodied the spirit of the Sixties and Seventies, however, left nonwhite women of the US aside and perpetuated a standard of femininity that did not account for the ethnic, economic, and social reality of the country. The mandates of female beauty (or nonbeauty), as well as the new paths that were opening for women in the country, were still noninclusive and perpetuated the Anglo, middle-class domination in the nation. The struggle of the *Chicana* feminists occurred and was exacerbated in this context of exclusion and invisibility. Aligning itself with many of the postulates of the white feminist movement, it added group-and class-specific issues to its demands, which accounted for and exposed the real ethnic and class diversity of the country.

5.3. *El Movimiento Chicano* and *la Chicana*

The emergence, development and achievements of the *Chicano* movement were, without doubt, the events that marked the most profound changes in the 'integration' of people of Mexican descent into the regular North American social arrangement during the 20th century. However, the rise of the movement was the conclusion of decades of struggle and ideological brewing, which fostered by the emergent civil right pleas, turned into what was called *El Movimiento*. Cynthia E. Orozco situates the beginning of the seeds of the ideology of the *Movimiento* back in the first decades of the 20th century, and she gives an example of how the middle-class Texas Mexicans had to shape their identity in relation to three different groups: the Anglo dominant class, the Mexican immigrants and the *Raza* working class (*No Mexicans* 40). The rejection of the first of the Mexican American community was obvious, as they were biasedly considered immigrants. The Mexican Americans, on the other hand, did not identify with either the newly arrived immigrants, whose nation was Mexico, or with the *Raza* working class, who aimed to relate to Mexico and spoke Spanish, despite their American citizenship. In this complex identification process, the Mexican Americans of the Twenties started to delineate an identity based on *mestizaje* and hybridity. Orozco describes how the Mexican political situation also altered the identification processes of the Mexican Americans, and events such as the Mexican Revolution, which brought abundant immigration into the United States, resulted in the growth of a feeling of fear and suspicion towards the Mexican stereotype of 'the bandit' and the subsequent militarization of the area. In this context, middle-class citizens aimed to stress their American citizenship and their belonging to the ethnosocial reality of the nation. Moreover, the different steps the US government took in the 'Americanization' of all citizens, the contradictory policy towards soldiers of Mexican origin and women in the workforce during World War I, and the construction of the 'Mexican problem' on their return, which questioned issues of belonging and citizenship of Mexican Americans, planted the seeds for the shaping of a Mexican American ideology that would in the ensuing decades struggle to reclaim a complex cultural and historical heritage that should be accepted as part of the US society. Said ideology began to be articulated in organizations such as LULAC (League of United Latin American Citizens), which was founded in February 1929 as a merger of several activist organizations focusing on the rights of people of Latin American origin in the United States. With regard to its constitutional text, LULAC defined its nature and demands, denounced racial discrimination, defended the racial origin of its members, deployed English as its language, vindicated citizenship, denounced worker abuse and, among other issues, "permitted female honorary members, but they could not vote on LULAC decisions" (Orozco, *No Mexicans* 169). As we have seen, the movement towards the recognition of people of Mexican descent (and other Latinos) in the United States did not account for female agency in its constituent steps. The women who worked in and for LULAC had to do it in the form of auxiliary members because

> [m]arriage, the division of labor, and reproduction could constrain women's participation. Husbands may not have wanted activist wives or may have disliked women's interaction with other men because of potential sexual relations. And they may have feared women's political education obtained through traveling and social interaction. Besides, women had to care for the family and home. Finally, political socialization prevented women from taking an active role. Religion and patriarchal family ideology kept politics a male domain. Prescriptive literature permeated the Spanish-language press and socialized women towards domesticity.
>
> (Orozco, *No Mexicans* 198)

Some five decades later, the *Chicano* movement of the Sixties also emerged as a predominantly male domain, and these women saw themselves in an obviously not better position than their predecessors in the 1920s. When analyzing the emergence and impact of the *Chicano* movement that occurred in the Sixties, it is essential to understand that its growth was also part of the spirit of a turbulent period in the United States. The Sixties became the culmination and explosion of diverse moves towards the acquisition of 'universal' freedom in the country, of the real materialization of the inherent 'pursuit of happiness' that the United States had based itself upon. Blacks, Native Americans, women, pacifists and of course *Chicanos* aimed to create a fairer society, where equal rights were guaranteed and finally implemented.

The political atmosphere in the country was boiling. The young, in particular, were eager for political commitment and renewal. With the Cold War as the international political heritage of the Fifties, the United States turned it into an active war by first sending 'advisors' and finally combat troops to Vietnam. This military participation provoked one of the greatest ideological divisions in the country ever. The assassination of J.F. Kennedy gave way to President Johnson's declaration that he would "make the United States into a 'great society' in which poverty and racial injustice had no place" ("The 1960s"). This aim could not be entirely fulfilled, and the incursion in Vietnam, together with the demands of the African Americans for full civil rights, gave rise to several organized movements, most of which arose from university campuses, and which demanded a fairer, more equal and pacifist country for all.

In this turbulent and change-demanding context, the Mexican American youth started establishing various and diverse organizations, and the "call for Chicanismo took on different meanings for different people. Generally, chicanismo meant both pride of identity and self-determination, in all their ambiguities" (Acuña 315). Some were based on the demands of those who had been dispossessed of their lands as a result of the division of the territory after the signing of the Treaty of Guadalupe Hidalgo, as was the case with the *New Mexican Farmers*, led by Reyes Tijerina. César Chávez and Dolores Huerta organized the *braceros* in California into several strikes and boycotts, under the umbrella of the United Farm Workers. Following these first steps, the urban *Chicano* movement initiated its organization, with the aim of demanding equal social and educational rights for the community. The activist Mexican American youth who joined the *Movimiento* were somewhat inspired by the already structured African American struggle and the upgrowing movements against the Vietnam War. The *Movimiento* was an urban mobilization, which started in colleges and campuses and called for equal opportunities for people of Mexican descent in the US social arrangement. Among its many vindications, the relevance of a proper education for kids became one of the axes of their fight. The social acceptance of their bilingual identity and their complex cultural heritage was part of their demand, and they put forward the idea that denying this fact was the source of high rates of educational failure and eventual social ostracism. The participants of the movement were first organized into diverse (mostly) student groups, including the MECHA (*Movimiento*

Estudiantil Chicano de Aztlán). Other factions also emerged, such as the Brown Berets, who, inspired by the Black Panthers, adopted a paramilitary style. The *Crusade for Justice*, on its part, delineated the *Plan de Espiritual de Aztlán*, which became the manifesto of the political agenda of the *Movimiento*. Later, the *Movimiento* would be organized into different groups, among which we need to highlight the *La Raza Unida Party*. All these struggles were inspired by an outgrowing feeling of cultural nationalism, *chicanismo*, which

> emphasized cultural pride as a source of political unity and strength capable of mobilizing *Chicanos* and *Chicanas* into an oppositional political group within the dominant political landscape of the United States. (. . .) *Chicano* cultural nationalism placed the socio-historical experiences of Mexican-Americans within a theoretical model of internal colonialism.
>
> (García 3)

This same notion of "internal colonialism" and the context of cultural nationalism represented the theoretical roots of *Chicana* feminism. Women, eager to defend their rights not only as part of the *Movimiento* but also as women, identified their discrimination and colonialism as being threefold, based on gender, sex and class. Inspired by the plight of their predecessors in the Mexican Revolution and adopting the postulates of the emerging feminist movement, the *Chicanas* of the Sixties and Seventies not only endeavored to vindicate ostracized and stereotyped figures such as *La Malinche*, but also tried to focus on the restructuring of gender-oppressive institutions such as the family, the clear machismo and male supremacy in their group, or the ever-mandating Catholic Church. Thus,

> [l]as feministas were vigorous in their demands for the Equal Rights Amendment, reproductive rights (safe birth control, legal abortion and no forced sterilization), fair divorce laws, sexual freedom, bilingual/bicultural childcare, nonracist and quality schools, welfare rights, and equality in hiring, education and credit. They also defended *Chicana*/o labor, undocumented workers, and prisoners, and they fought against racism, the Vietnam War, poverty, police brutality and suppression of *Chicana*/o culture and the Spanish language. By preserving the conviction that the fight against race and sex oppression was inseparable, they helped forge the widespread acceptance of that idea today.
>
> (Alaniz & Cornish 250)

As can be seen in the above words, the women of the Sixties were essentially and consciously activists, who participated in the vast array of equal rights movements that were occurring simultaneously and interconnectedly in the United States in the Sixties. Among the most prominent *Chicana* organizations of the time, the work of MUJER will be taken as an example in the following lines, as a clear illustration of the range and depth of the demands of these women: "it promoted *Chicana* issues, offered a female viewpoint on the *Chicana*/o community, and promoted *Chicana* and Mexicana leadership. MUJER raised funds for college scholarships for *Chicanas*, opposed forced sterilization, and supported abortion rights and gay liberation" (Alaniz & Cornish 267).

Many of the above-mentioned issues were regarded as a direct affront to the traditional roots of the *Chicano* community, and thus clashed both with *Chicano* cultural nationalism as a concept and with the *Movimiento* as a reality. The idea of a female collective that would decide on the reproductive choices provided by the emerging contraceptive methods, for instance, was clearly interpreted as a betrayal of the group. In this context, Alma M. García posits that "a common trope found in many of the basic writings by *Chicana* feminists is the recognition that the existence and perpetuation of patriarchy represents an essential source of women's oppression" (6). Their position as feminist women of color found fierce opposition not only from the men in the *Movimiento* but also from white feminists, who defended sexism as the only source of the universal discrimination of women, regardless of class and ethnic issues. At the National *Chicano* Youth Conference in 1969, "no resolution was proposed to deal with the issue of gender inequality. A handful of *Chicana* feminists organized a *Chicana* workshop for the purpose of drafting a resolution on the subject" (Muñoz, C. 93). But when the conference delegates reconvened to vote on all the resolutions that emerged from the workshops, the representative of the *Chicana* caucus reported that "it was the consensus of the group that the *Chicana* does not want to be liberated" (Longueaux y Vasquez, qtd. in Muñoz, C. 93). Moreover, as Adelaida R. Del Castillo describes in La Visión *Chicana*, the relationship with Anglo women was a complicated one. For her, the postulates of the Anglo liberation movement raise questions such as: "Do we as *Chicanos* and *Chicanas* want to advance and work in this system, this capitalistic system? Does capitalism perpetrate welfare, racism, sexism? Does it perpetrate our poverty? Does it profit from it? Then, if it does, we have to start considering what alternatives are open for us" (46).

The essence of the discrimination against *Chicanas*, according to the first *Chicana* feminists, was not only sexism but also class differences and racism. Their struggle was thus multifaceted and had to be confronted from various standpoints. In the same vein, the source of their gender underprivilege was deeply rooted in the religious and historical tradition of their community, which was similarly complex and varied. Anna Nieto-Gómez, for instance, states that this discrimination derives from the colonization of Mexico. In fact,

> [t]he roots of the psyche of la *Chicana* lies deep within the colonial period in Mexico. The conquest, the encomienda system and the colonial Catholic Church were to play a major role in forming the sexual-social roles of the Mexican woman. And the class relationship between patrón and the Indian slave woman provides the historical foundation of the machismo phenomenon. Rape of the Mexican Indian women by the Spanish conquistadores was an act of conquest and marriage subsequently became a tool of colonization. Rape and marriage represented models for the Mexican male who longed to be free and strong like the conquistadores.
>
> ("La Chicana" 49)

She continues to expose the negative influence the Church exerted upon the construction of the identity of the *Chicana* by defining the conquest as a positive tool, as well as by imposing the veneration of the *Virgen de Guadalupe, Marianismo*. This image defined the female 'proper' identity mirroring her as a mother, martyr, wife, sex object, and virgin. In her essay "Sexism in the *Movimiento*," the scholar goes on to say that the colonization has affected both *Chicanos* and *Chicanas*, who all suffer racist sexism. Thus, "colonized men of color are considered as inferior as women since colonized men do not have the power or authority to rule, provide economically and protect the family. (. . .) The colonized women of color are considered more passive, dependent, and childlike than women of the superior race. (. . .) Her skills and abilities are centered around her sexual prowess, and procreation." (98)

In this context of self- and social denial, as well as opposition from the men of the *Movimiento*, who considered their vindications an affront to the group and an imitation of the white ways, the *Chicanas* were organized into several groups that demanded their rights. Similarly, they theorized and wrote about their condition, creating an emerging and growing *Chicana* feminist thought, which endeavored to erase the stereotypes and define a new, evolving, contemporary *Chicana* self, which would account for the complexity of the Mexican American woman's discrimination, on the one hand, and her cultural and historical heritage, on the other.

The *Chicana* feminist movement was active in practical and conceptual spheres, and gave rise to a whole set of artistic representations and discourses that are still considered contemporary today and are read and studied internationally. The *Chicana* feminist movement and its participants were thus intellectually active women, who demanded a communal and individual voice, as well as an active, agentic participation both in their own life choices and in the social realm. The marches and rallies, meetings and caucuses marked the agenda of these women, who stepped out and called for 'a street of their own.'

In this context, I find the role that personal image, self-image, and public identity acquired for these voiced women extremely interesting. Undoubtedly, the Sixties were a time of revolution in terms of propriety, sexual conduct and roles, and provided the ground for the breaking of norms and moral values that had not been questioned up to that moment. The *Chicanas*, as active members of the changes to come during the civil rights era, aligned with the times and provided a break with "their puritanical mode of dress. (. . .) They are no longer afraid to show their intellect, their capabilities and their potential" (Chávez 38). The obviously voiced, political agenda of these women, and the need to break with the roles assigned to them during centuries of oppression, brought these women to subvert the norms of the female code of style and conduct, in a way that was different to the other two groups of women focused upon in this study: *Pachucas* and *Cholas*.

5.4. The *Chicana* style politics

The *Chicana* movement, as explained before, was articulated around (or against) the influence of both the *Chicano* and the feminist movement that emerged in the Sixties.

Regardless of the fact that there is not a homogeneous *Chicana* style, it is true that *Chicanas* adopted a style that was contemporary to the one prevalent in the Sixties and was somehow influenced by the natural, free hippie one that was predominant among the young people of the period. The *Chicana* feminist movement, coetaneous to both this hippie movement and the feminist liberation one, had, among its plights, the vindication of the body as a personal marker of identity and as a site of individual emancipation. The tenets of the feminist liberation movement, regardless of the obvious ideological differences that existed between these two groups (each of which, once again, may not be regarded as homogeneous), were adopted by the *Chicana* feminist activists, who fought for their liberation from a too-male chauvinistic and traditional set of communal values. The need to redescribe and redefine what a woman's role within the community was often demonstrated through the redescription and redefinition of traditional values, which had ascribed women to very strict sets of moral and behavioral codes. Thus, the epitome of the good woman, *La Virgen de Guadalupe*, not only showed how a woman should act, her necessary passive and submissive attitude towards life in general, and her counterparts in particular, but also established what the code of decency was for women.

La Virgen de Guadalupe, as portrayed in most of its different, yet similar representations, is always presented as a woman whose body is covered from head to toes, her hair hidden underneath her tunic, and who shows no hint of apparent physicality. The richly ornamented, beautiful and colorful tunic that covers her and transmits a certain sense of joy and happiness due to said colors, however, is conceived to cover her body fully, and only her face and hands are shown in public. These, moreover, depict quietude and peacefulness, but also submissiveness. The Virgin's head, looking down and not facing to the front, inclined in an obedient, compliant fashion, shows no trace of agency or personal empowerment. Similarly, her praying, still hands portray no activity whatsoever and clearly represent a woman's subservient acceptance of her traditional role.

This representation of womanhood and femininity was obviously contested by the first *Chicana* activists, who, with their clearly articulated political discourse, defied said traditional roles and sought a self-defined identity, grounded on the basis of common civil rights and human equality. Among the most relevant vindications of this collective, we should, once again, highlight each woman's right to control her own body, in the personal and communal sense of it. A woman's sexual choice, therefore, was her own choice, and her body was no longer understood as a communal tool through which the preservation and perpetuation of the community was ensured.

In this context, it is interesting to observe the way the body and its external appearance in the form of physical look (that is, clothing, makeup, hairstyle, ornaments in general and finally demeanor and physical stance) was used by these highly activist and politically conscious women. Bearing in mind that the previous chapter stated that *Pachucas* created *subversion and deviation through the unconscious*, the following lines will be devoted to showing the way the *Chicanas*' deviation was articulated and performed in the public sphere. The chapter aims to demonstrate whether physical appearance and bodily posture and demeanor were valid means of contestation for a group of women whose political discourse was already a direct and fierce affront to the mandates of both the mainstream society and their own community, too traditional and constraining regarding gender roles. For this purpose, I will look at the implications of the performative role of dress and attitude in two groups of *Chicana* activists: the Brown Berets and the *Chicana* feminists.

5.4.1. The Brown Berets

The Brown Berets were formed as an organization in the year 1966 and disappeared as such in 1973. During these years of activism and protests, the Brown Berets focused primarily on the poor educational system for young people of Mexican and Latino origin, and more particularly on the "poor facilities, lack of books, and charges of racism among administrators and teachers" (Correa 89). The Brown Berets emerged from a previous movement called the Young Citizens for Community Action (YCCA), and organized themselves in the fashion of the African American Black Panthers. They had "titles like Prime Minister, Minister of Communications, Finance, Recruitment, Training, etc. (. . .) membership in the Brown Berets was based only on racial background (Mexican) and apparent commitment (hanging around)" (Fields 134). The look they adopted was highly homogenizing and consisted of a brown military uniform that represented unity and strength, as well as a defensive attitude, and a highly symbolic Brown Beret, positioned in an inclined way over the member's head. Their demeanor and organizational practice were militaristic and their aim was to transmit the idea of discipline, commitment, and strength.

Their constitutional manifesto, written by Prime Minister David Sánchez at the Wayside Maximum Security Los Angeles County Jail in February 1968 (Fields 282), establishes the norms and regulations of the organization, the total commitment to *La Causa* expected from its members and their duties and obligations. Their foundational pledge, moreover, points at the relevance of the beret as a symbol of strength, pride and unity. It says:

> "As a member of the Brown Beret Organization, I have committed myself to be a dedicated, sincere servant to my community, and my people, by all means necessary, therefore, it is an absolute must that I conduct myself in a mature manner, at all times. I must remember that I am a Brown Beret twenty-four (24) hours a day." "When I wear the Brown Beret hat, I am wearing the beret to symbolize unity. Therefore, I cannot let my personal problems or conflicts interfere in my line of duty. I wear the beret because I realize the dignity and how proud I am in the color of my skin and race."
>
> (Fields 290)

The brown beret, as observed in the above words, not only serves as a symbol of pride and unity, but also as a unifying, homogenizing, identifying mark of belonging to *La Causa* in general, and the Berets in particular. Similarly, the military uniform provides its members with no hint of individuality or personal agency as they serve the world and their fellow *Chicanos* in a communal, nonpersonal, altruistic way. In this sense, the image and attitude of the Brown Berets were diametrically opposed to the hippie and feminist liberation movements that were occurring in parallel, which were aimed at celebrating personal, free expression, devoid of the constraining moral and social mandates of the mainstream status quo.

Similarly, the women Brown Berets adopted the norms of style and behavior imposed upon all the members of the group, which included the uniformization, both physically and conceptually, of its members. The presence of the women in the Brown Berets was a reality, but in general terms, we can affirm that the Berets were a predominantly male and patriarchal organization. As occurred with the *Movimiento Chicano*, in general, the Brown Berets sought and fought for social equality but failed to include the rights and agency of women within their plight. Professor Dionne Espinoza affirms that:

> [t]he organization's structure, which originally appeared to support participatory democracy, albeit in tension with paramilitary procedures and self-representations, progressively devolved into the segregation and subordination of women in the drive toward aggressive and violent masculinity.
>
> (22)

The scholar argues that this segregation, which the women endured for the first years, was the catalyst for their abandonment of the Brown Berets and their subsequent organization into *Las Adelitas de Aztlan* as *Hermanas en La Lucha*, forming an all-women group where institutionalized gender segregation did not exist. Most of the tasks that women performed in the Brown Berets were office ones, leaving the most public ones for the male members of the group. The Berets arranged a *barrio*-free clinic that was fully organized and maintained by the women Berets. But in sum, "patriarchal gender roles were also part of the daily lives of the Brown Beret organization (and the overall *Chicano* movement), as female Berets experienced sexism and an inferior perception by male members" (Correa 94).

Similarly to their male counterparts, the Brown Beret women had to adapt to strict codes of personal appearance, and purity and strength were two of the main concepts that their attire and demeanor sought to express. Ethnographer Rona Fields describes the relationship of the Berets with the fashion mores in the following terms:

> In fashion and entertainments the Brown Berets are quite oriented to the Anglo middle-class mores. Although some of the girls disregard it, they have been pressured against wearing slacks and shorts, and against adopting very short mini-skirts and sheer blouses – though these are commonly worn by their Anglo peers.
>
> For parties and organizational functions there is a uniform for the girls. It is a long gown with a square neck and long, flowing sleeves. The pattern is a

very simple A-Line, and there is trim at the neck and cuffs of the sleeves. The material is either brown or gold.

(201–11)

The description of not only the attire but also the strict regulations imposed upon the women of the organization proves the group's evident control of gender roles and supports an obvious gender supremacy on the part of the male members. The regular uniform is aimed at showing women as pure, decent, politically engaged women. Their look and general attitude were diametrically opposed to the *Pachucas'* exaggerated and hyperfeminized one, and tried to avoid the negative impact that their short skirts provoked among the members of both the mainstream and the Mexican American communities. Similarly, this need to cover the body, and especially at parties and communal celebrations, recalls the description provided above of *La Virgen de Guadalupe*'s tunic, where the body is covered completely, providing the Virgin (and the Brown Beret women) with a nonsexualized image, which deprives her of any bodily agency or control. As stated before, the rigid code of behavior and of the way the external appearance of the Berets should be is heightened in the case of the women, whose bodies seem to also belong to the group. However, and as Fields says, there was sexual promiscuity among the Berets, which "evolves out of party behaviors, but there is considerable effort made to 'cover.' These are not the 'sexual freedom generation' of their age peers in Anglo society. There is concern about and wanting to be 'a nice girl'" (209).

Deriving from this intra-groupal set of relationships, marriages among the Brown Berets occurred and similarly the participants had to respond to a set of codes of behavior and appearance that would still connect them to the community they belonged to, which had to continuously present a sense of unbreakable unity. Espinoza describes the attire adopted by the members in the following words:

> Many *Chicanas* had come to the organization as independent women who embraced the agenda of the Brown Berets, and they affirmed – and creatively developed – their commitment to recovering the indigenous, which was a strong current in the revaluing of racial-ethnic identity. All of the core members were bridesmaids or bridegrooms in the wedding. While the men wore the uniform of bush jacket and khaki pants, the bridesmaids – all Beret women – designed a modified version of the huipil, the traditional garment sewn and embroidered by indigenous Mexican women. These they wore in conjunction with the stylish stacked hairstyles and heavy mascara that clearly situated them in the late Sixties.
>
> (27)

The adoption of indigenous symbols as a mark of ethnic pride and the vindication of an indigenous heritage prior to the arrival of the Spanish colonizers in the mid-15th century connects the Brown Beret women to an idealized indigenous past, an idea that was placed at the core of the *Chicano* nationalist discourse of the *Movimiento*. However, as Espinoza affirms,

> while the desire to claim their connection to indigenous Mexican women was motivated by antiracism and had the potential to tap into an argument for egalitarianism as a feature of precolonial society (an argument that became prevalent during the *Chicana* feminist movement despite its equivocal aspects), the women did not yet have access to the information that would have enabled such a reading.
>
> (27)

This indigenization of the female Beret in particular and of the *Chicana* activist in general became a recurrent trope in the *Chicano* nationalist discourse. The vindication of the mythical territory of Aztlán, where the indigenous roots of the *Chicanos* were to be found, became a relevant demand of the *Movimiento*, who adopted a clear anti-colonial stance that looked back at the Spanish Conquista of the Aztec territories and the subjugation and dismantling of the empire. In the case of women, the adoption and reinforcement of a clear indigenous look by means of the attire the female activists wore, as well as through the strengthening of individual indigenous traits (such as the long, dark hair), became a sign of identity that also connected the activists to their group, and hence to *La Causa*. In the case of the Brown Berets, because of their strict code of behavior and attire, the women's hair became a symbol of racial pride and unity, and the women Berets reinforced this aspect of their body and look. A clear symbol of this fact is Raul Ruiz picture of a Brown Beret (soldier) wearing a bandolier, which becomes not only a revolutionary symbol but also an adornment, and the very identifiable brown beret.

The photograph, taken by Raul Ruiz and first published in *La Verdad* magazine in the early Seventies has become an iconic symbol of the female Brown Berets and can be found at various written and digital sources. In it, we can observe a female Brown Beret in a highly central position, regardless of the fact that the image shows there is a man to her left and a woman in the back. The photograph portrays a medium shot of a female Brown Beret, sitting in a seemingly relaxed position. The young woman is looking to her left, directing her gaze at somebody/something, but not necessarily at the man to her left. She is a young woman and her facial characteristics define her as 'stereotypically brown and mestiza.' Regardless of the fact that the photograph is slightly cut from the top, a brown beret can be easily recognizable, and thus, identifies her with this organization. Her eyes and her long hair are dark, attributes which, once again, connect her to an 'stereotypically indigenous' look. She is a young, feminine, Brown (beret) woman. But what definitely, in my view, stands out in this photograph is the crossed bandoliers that she is wearing in her chest on top of a sleeveless, plain, top. These are formed by high caliber rifle bullets, some of which seem used, some others 'ready to be used.' The symbolic meaning of the bandoliers is, undoubtedly, revolutionary and (probably) aggressive, and moreover, connect this woman, and hence, the Brown Beret movement in general to other organizations and popular movements which were openly adopting militaristic 'solutions' both in the US and outside its borders. Namely, the Black Panthers in the United States and most of the communist-inspired revolutionary movements in Central and South America. In fact, both the beret and the bandoliers recall the similarly iconic image of the world widely influential Che Gevara. The mixture of a relaxed, feminine figure (for hegemonic patriarchal gender standards) and the symbolical use of the bullet bandoliers, served a purpose and the photograph circulated widely. It is, in fact, today, an image that comes to the public's mind when thinking about the female Brown Berets. This same woman was photographed by George Rodriguez, probably in the same day, looking to the front and looking directly to the camera. This medium shot, once again, shows the woman alone, but in this take, we can observe there are political posters behind her. Both of them are related to *La Raza*, and connect her directly to the fight for *La Causa*. This shot, a little ampler than Ruiz's photograph, enhances the woman's femininity (the top she is wearing looks similar to a dress in it) and her indigeneity.

Both photographs depict a role model for Brown Beret women in particular and *Chicana* activists in general, and represent a revolutionary woman, who embodies all the physical and attitudinal traits an activist should have. However, and according to scholar Dionne Espinoza when she analyzes Raul Ruiz's iconic photograph, it also conveys once more the utilization of the woman's body and identity as a symbol of a pre-established role, and leaves no room for female agency. Just as the most traditional values of both the Mexican and the Mexican American culture represented and defended a clear-cut set of values and beliefs in relation to a woman's position and proper role, the image of the Brown Beret activist also promoted a very specific role in terms of racial and gender identification of women. The scholar says:

> The photo shows a *mestiza revolucionaria* with crossed bandoliers and long-flowing hair. Simply put, while the woman in the photo represents a type of beauty that the movement would celebrate in contrast to the dominant culture – that is, mestizo beauty in contrast to blond hair and blue eyes – it also features a femininity appealing to men and offers an ideal for *Chicanas* to consider as they pursued social change. Such an image (. . .) fits within the tradition of portraying women as representatives of nation and embodiments of revolution, their bodies standing for what is at stake – a way of life, biological and cultural reproduction – as well as a reminder that there was a role for everyone to play in the collective effort to claim the notion.
>
> (27)

The appropriation of the woman's image and of her life and destiny was evident in the case of the Berets, just like that of the male members of the organization. The paramilitary essence of the group, together with the obvious defense of communal aims and targets, left little room for individual choice. In the case of women, this control was exacerbated by the clear hierarchical kind of gender relationships that occurred within the organization, which were soon identified by the women as oppressive and planted the seeds for the eventual abandonment of the women Berets of the group and their quest for another line of struggle, as expressed in Brown Beret Gloria Arellanes' *testimonio* to Chicano historian Mario T. García (156-157). As previously stated, the control over the women was not only ideological but also physical and attitudinal, and had a direct relationship with the look the women had to present. Other visual accounts of the times which show the Berets in military formation display the absolute masculinization of the female Berets, who adopted fully masculine military attire and who were, therefore, integrated into the common, externally ungendered army of Brown Berets. These images provide a clear visual representation of the unification and homogenization of the Brown Beret soldiers, who adopted an overtly military pose and attitude and were organized as such. The women in the military lines are, at first glance, regarded as equals and at the same hierarchical level as their male peers, but they nevertheless experienced clear segregation when it came to the division of roles and tasks, as has been observed previously. In terms of their physical appearance, the female Berets were left no choice of individual performance and the military uniform became the only possibility in regard to external expression. In the case of women, the long hair also seems a requirement, and most of the women in the army wore this symbol of femininity, on the one hand, and indigeneity, on the other. In sum, the long dark hair turned into a racialized and genderized symbol that distinguished the female Berets from their male peers.

The Brown Beret women's gradual acquisition of a feminine communal voice and their demand for female agency within the group culminated in their abandonment of the organization, but previously had marked a difference. The Brown Beret women chose, first, not to wear the uniform, and then to create their own version of the military outfit, which included a short black skirt. Gloria Arellanes, probably the most relevant female Brown Beret, who eventually became Minister of Finance, affirms that "We stayed very feminine – and wanted to" (Espinoza 28).

In this line, the external change of the adoption of the skirt within the uniform is evident and provides the Brown Beret female look and attitude with a highly complex set of symbolic signification. Photographs that show the female Berets in military formation with skirts show the conscious acceptance of the military (and hence highly hierarchical and masculine) pose and symbolic arrangement. The women Berets line up like soldiers and their static, erratic pose clashes, in my view, with the short black miniskirt, which in the Sixties represented a step towards female liberation, the free exposition of the female body and, in sum, personal agency and choice. Similarly, some of the visual representations of the moment prove that the boots of the female Brown Berets are no longer military ones, but those that were fashionable for women wearing miniskirts in the Sixties. It is interesting to note, however, that the female Berets opted for wearing the very masculine and thus caste military jacket of the uniform, as well as, of course, the beret, which identified them as active members of the group and symbolically connected them to other revolutions that had occurred or were occurring, mostly in South and Central American neighboring countries. Moreover, probably coincidentally, the women in these photographs no longer seem to have the very long, free hair that the previous photos portrayed, but have adopted diverse and personal looks, which, in general, were devoid of the racial identification that the dark long hair encompassed. The changes, in sum, were a step towards the "liberation" of the female Brown Berets, as expressed by Espinoza:

> (But) despite the existence of a soldadera frame that could co-opt them into a masculinist imaginary (an imaginary that was also taken by *Chicanas* in a very reductive, complex, and/or woman-identified ways . . .) (. . .), *Chicana* Berets constructed a revolutionary identity while negotiating the constellation of already existing cultural representations and societal positioning of *Chicanas*, the demands of a paramilitary organization and its specific gendering practices (explicit and implicit), and their own self-conception as shaped by personal experience and a growing knowledge of mestiza history. Out of this intersection of forces, they opted, at various times, to work within – and eventually to rework and reject – the terms mapped out for them.
> (28)

In sum, during the years the women Berets were part of the organization, the control they endured was firm and constraining. These women, conscious of what belonging to a paramilitary organization implied, followed the mandates of the (male) group, but were subject to a strong gender submission and acceptance of demeaning roles. Among other issues related to behavioral codes and relationship mores, the control over the physical appearance of these women was obvious and put them in the position of the women of previous generations, whose bodies served the community for various purposes. The Brown Berets, with their homogeneous uniform and gender and racialized identities, became the symbols of a nationalist, paramilitary organization, which once again utilized women (until they opted to abandon the situation) for communal purposes.

For the aim of this volume, the Brown Beret organization, and the women Brown Berets, provide an interesting standpoint, which differs greatly from the previously analyzed one of *Pachucas* in the Forties. The conscious and committed participation of the women in the organization, which implied the subsequent voluntary acceptance of its rigid codes of behavior and morality, could be understood as a clear move of contestation against the status quo. The Brown Berets, therefore, adopted a *conscious position of subversion and deviance through the conscious* and their physical appearance and military demeanor became a direct affront and symbolic rejection of mainstream rules and society. Their move towards a homogeneous identity, devoid of any personal traits, on the contrary, positioned them in a situation of invisibility and nothingness towards that same community that they tried to defend themselves against. Moreover, the uniformization of both the men and the women within the group favored the hierarchization of the organization as well as the existence of a clear binary axis around which the group evolved: men and women. This division, grounded on clear hierarchical roots, positioned the Brown Beret women in a situation of inferiority that recalled and reproduced the very clear patriarchal norms that were prevalent (and had become the target of the emerging feminist movement) both in the mainstream society and the Mexican American one. This plight was adopted by women who became activists in the *Chicana* feminist movement, and who, in contrast to the Brown Beret women, sought a holistic female liberation, which accounted for social, economic and sexual freedom and agency.

5.4.2. The Chicana *feminist activists*

Undoubtedly, the emergence of the *Movimiento Chicano*, of *La Causa*, brought with it a profound revision of the role of *Chicanos* within the intricate sociocultural and ethnic panorama of the United States. Similarly, it suggested a redescription of Mexican American and *Chicano* history, which would recover elements of an indigenous past that had been erased by centuries of ethnic and sociocultural colonization. During the *Movimiento* years, the demand for fair and just civil rights for all members of the North American society became the axis around which the Movement was articulated, in a way parallel to other civil rights movements and organizations that were booming in the United States. Better educational and labor opportunities, the recognition of a specific cultural and linguistic heritage and, in sum, a voice within society were the main goals of the *Movimiento*. A highly masculine movement in its incipient stages, the status quo regarding the division of roles according to gender and the obvious secondary position of women in the public sphere (both in the mainstream and that of the community) were not part of the political agenda of the Movement.

In this context, the voices of women were not accounted for, nor were their demands for sexual freedom, birth control and the public participation of women in social and educational institutions as full members of society. Considered a threat to the community's stability, the *Movimiento*'s male peers reacted in a highly sexist way to the women's demands, as described by Cynthia Orozco (1990, qtd. in Flores):

> The efforts of these *Chicana* feminists of the early 1970s were received with mixed reactions by a community that was being reconstructed both by the *Chicano* cultural nationalists and the *Chicana* activists. As *Chicana* feminists, the women nonetheless adhered to the general goals of the *Chicano* movement even as they attempted to give greater equality to the women of their culture. *Chicana* feminist historian Cynthia Orozco identifies four sexist reactions that emerged out of the *Chicano* movement in regard to *Chicana* feminism: "I) 'El problema es el gabacho, no el macho.' (The problem is white people, not the Anglo male). 2) Feminism was Anglo, middle-class, and bourgeois. 3) Feminism was a diversion from the 'real' and 'basic' issues, that is, racism and class exploitation. 4) Feminism sought to destroy 'la familia,' supposedly the base of Mexican culture and the basis for resistance to domination."

(37)

These four claims show an obvious need for control and maintenance of the hierarchical status quo within the community and minimized the *Chicanas'* complex source of discrimination, part of which they shared with their male counterparts, but this was aggravated by the strong patriarchal tradition that the community relied on. Assuming that women were the bearers of the tradition and thus their role was that of perpetuating the community (and its traditional gender division), *Chicano* activists and many women defended the idea that women's place was at the domestic sphere, which would allow to provide the men enough spare time to be active in the *Movimiento* and in the public struggle of the community (Orozco, *No Mexicans* 205–6). For the first feminist thinkers, however, "true liberation required a feminist base" (Bebout 140), and the revision of a centuries-long subjugation of women in the name of tradition and the maintenance of the community's values that originated from pre-Columbian times (Cotera 1976) were essential for the group's social and cultural freedom.

The domination of women and their relegation to the domestic sphere was directly related to the lack of control over their bodies, and thus of their reproductive possibilities. Similarly, the patriarchal rule in general, and its performance by men in particular, was put into practice by a strong set of behavioral and attitudinal rules and others related to the external, public image that women had to/could transmit. As previously mentioned, the very well-established traditional history, based on strongly assimilated myths such as *La Virgen de Guadalupe, La Malinche* and/or *La Llorona*, easily permeated said rules throughout the *Chicano* and Mexican American population. Similarly to the image of the *Virgen, La Llorona* represents a submissive, enduring, passive woman, a suffering being whose voice is silenced by her grief. Regardless of the fact that the representations of *La Llorona* are various and diverse throughout different geographical areas and cultural traditions, she is very often represented as a virginal woman, who, once again, shows no trace of physicality.

La Malinche, on the other hand, is portrayed as a generally more physical (and even sexual) female figure, whose voice and agency doomed her to eternal condemnation on the part of her community, due to her supposed betrayal of the group and the subsequent defeat and disappearance of the Aztec Empire. However, this woman, agentic, active and with a voice, was recovered and vindicated by *Chicana* feminist activists as a role model. The first representations of *La Malinche* date back to the codex that describes the arrival of the Spaniards and the final seizing and defeat of the Aztec Empire. After that, the different and sometimes differing representations of *La Malinche*, such as in the mural at the Palacio Nacional de Méjico by Diego Rivera, always present them, in contrast to the *Virgen de Guadalupe*, as a more physical and corporeal woman. Her role as a translator also defines her as a woman with a voice of her own and she was accordingly recovered by *Chicana* feminists as an active, voiced woman. Her beauty, bodily ornamentation through feathers and beads and her tattooed body depict her as a sexualized woman, in contrast to the virginal, static, submissive representation of the *Virgen de Guadalupe*. Moreover, her central position in the mural and her outstanding white dress define her as a woman whose gender role and the expectations that accompany it do not stop her from participating actively in the community's social life. She is surrounded by indigenous men who are defined as 'savages' (one of them is carrying a human arm) and probably aggressive, but her attitude is one of centrality, quietude and self-confidence.

Leaving aside the many social and cultural vindications that the *Chicana* feminists proposed in their political agenda, actions and writings, it is my aim to draw some general, personal conclusions about the way these women contested the established moral and attitudinal codes (both of the mainstream group and the *Chicano* one) through their physical, symbolical, body language, that is, through their clothes and attitude, or, in sum, their style. Given the fact that these women possessed and articulated themselves a strong political discourse, that is, they performed an obvious and direct *subversion and deviation through the conscious*, I consider it interesting to examine whether the body and its public presentation as a tool of contestation helped accomplish said deviant and contestational attitude. In Irene Blea's words,

> [f]or striving toward a different society, *Chicanas* were frequently thought of as deviant. Women who had wanted to change traditional gender roles, the socialization process, and gender-typed opportunities for women are often thought of as deviant; they are not normal, but somehow strange. Generally, social deviance is measured by the degree to which individuals differ from those who conform to the norms: an Anglo norm, a *Chicano* norm, and norms for women in both of these groups.
>
> (9)

Fully aligning myself with Blea's notion of the deviation of *Chicanas*, I would add, however, that *Chicana* activists, and particularly the feminist ones, were not only regarded as deviant by the already mentioned social forces, but, most importantly, they considered themselves deviant and acted in deviant ways. One way of demonstrating such deviance and subversion was, as will be seen, their physical appearance and personal attitude.

Chicano photographer Jesus Manuel Mena Garza's picture "Chicano Park" is, in my view, a clear representation of these women's conscious deviant attitude and physical image and moods. Before delving deeper into the matter, however, I consider it necessary to clarify that the observations that will be articulated hereafter are not applicable to all women (and men) who were part of the *Chicano* movement, nor are the descriptions and conclusions that will be provided aimed at categorizing or labeling them. The analysis of certain pictures recovered from different sources will be aimed at drawing some general conclusions on the role of clothing and physical attitude in the quest for a personal identity, which was a key issue in the case of the *Chicana* activists, and, moreover, in the search for a 'different, deviant' voice that stated clearly that things had to change in society (both the mainstream and their own) for women to be able to accomplish their demands.

The black and white photograph which can be seen in various Chicano/a-oriented web pages and printed material, as well as in the author's personal online portfolio, is part of a collection which the author compiled in the year 2013 and portray the Chicano community of San José, California, from the years 1970-1975. This particular photograph shows three young Chicanos/as in a natural setting which seems a park, HELLYER Park in San José, posing to the camera with (their) a car. The one sitting on the wheel of the car stands in the back of the photograph, in a dark position, and it is difficult to recognize, even if he looks like a boy, but her two friends are closer to the camera and could be be identifiable as young Chicanas (even if one of them looks ambiguous in terms of gender, and could be a young man). In any case, one of them is sitting in the car seat, with her crossed legs outside the car, looking to the front and smoking a cigarette. She has dark eyes and long, black hair, and thus, looks, 'brown.' She is wearing a light top, which is tight and short in the waist, and thus, looks like a 'femenine' one. From the image, we can infer she is wearing elephant- leg jeans and a white, big belt, which once again, probably rendered her with a very Sixties, hippie, 'womanly' look. There is a third young person/woman in the image who is standing, looking towards the right of the setting, and thus, not facing the camera directly. I would here like to clarify that there is no clear physical evidence of her being a woman taking into account the male/female physical binary, as she can be described as 'manly.' In any case, I recognize her as female (observing her hands and eyes) and in that sense, I consider s/he is symbolic of the erasure of gender barriers in terms of physical appearance that the hippie and feminist revolutions brought along with them. Similarly, this photograph also allows me to prove that said gender binary is based on a set of physical traits which have been attributed to males and females as 'inherent and natural,' and which can be challenged, as the person in the photograph shows. Regardless of the fact that I recognize her as a woman, if she were a man, he would also be challenging the gender norms expected from him by both the mainstream society and their own group, the Chicano society. She (he) is also smoking and with her other hand, she is holding a folded paper. Even if s/he is not looking directly at the camera, we can infer she also has dark eyes and her/his hair is much longer and 'less taken-care-of,' 'more natural,' than her/his friends'. This hair provides her/him with a highly indigenous look. Her clothes also differ from her friends', and she looks 'masculine.' She is dressed in dark clothes, with a long-sleeved black (masculine) shirt and a dark vest on top. She is wearing some dark Levi's wide-legged jeans. It is interesting to note that at the bottom end of the jeans, they show a patch (probably meant to fix a hole in them) with the logo *Chicano Power* in them. Both are wearing, plain, black comfortable lace-up-shoes.

    The photograph, which shows these self-conscious, free, young *Chicana/os* may well represent the demand for agency and a new voice that the women of their time demonstrated, in this case, by a clearly opposing attitude to that of the *Virgen de Guadalupe or La Llorona*. The picture depicts three young Chicanas/os, who, through their poses, actions and physical look, defy and consciously reject the roles that the *Chicano* community, and that of the mainstream, expected from them. The fact that they are sitting in a car is, to start with, obviously challenging. The photograph shows them in a car, and hence we understand that they drove to the setting where the picture was taken, regardless of the fact that there is no evidence that the women own the car, as the person in the wheel seems to be a man. However, both the fact that they are in a park and that they have driven there is a symbol of the fact that they have crossed the border of their bedrooms (McRobbie) and have left the domestic space to become active members of society. The appropriation of an obviously masculine symbol such as the car by these young women is, in itself, a revolutionary symbol, which expresses the freedom and need for personal emancipation that these women were seeking, and supposedly, as seen in the picture, had attained. Similarly, the fact that two of them are smoking and do it looking at the camera, and are consciously convinced that what they are doing is licit, portrays, once again, that they have clearly crossed the border of masculine/feminine expectations and rights. They, as human beings with the right to make choices, choose to smoke regardless of what is expected of them. The symbolic meaning of this act and their attitude is evident and the effect provoked by it on a Mexican American traditional public in the Seventies was probably one of concern and alarm. Finally, the attire of the two women in the front is worth mentioning, and once again it is symbolic of female agency and individual choice, devoid of the strict norms of behavior and decency that women were subjected to. The young woman on the left, standing on the car, can be described as almost 'stereotypically attitudinally' masculine. Her long hair, in the tradition of the women Berets we have dealt with previously, is a symbol of femininity and indigeneity, but in this particular case is challenged by the girl's almost 'masculine pose' (taking into account patriarchal parameters and standards). Her big, loose denim pants respond to the mores of the hippie fashion of the time, in which elephant leg pants were popular. However, their obviously big size leaves the woman with a lack of femininity, which, together with her pose, the fact that she is smoking and not looking at the camera, and her general bodily posture and attitude, depicts her, in my view, as a rebel who defies the norms, rules and roles that she is probably expected to fulfill. Finally, the dark vest reinforces the previously described almost masculine pose and look, and frames her as a cowboy/cowgirl, ready for action. In sum, her physical image does not reveal her gender, and she could be recognized as a male or a female young Chicano/a. The second woman, similarly smoking and looking directly at the camera, shows no hint of shame in her attitude and actions, but on the contrary seems secure and convinced in front of the camera. Like her peer, she is wearing the pants in fashion in the Sixties but seems more feminine (once again, according to patriarchal standards) than her friend. Her hair is shorter and, thus, less 'indigenous' and she is wearing a blouse that shapes her figure and provides her with a fashionable, contemporary-to-the-times, look and attitude. Their makeup-free faces, moreover, depict these women as free from the mandates and obligations related to female beauty and the depiction of femininity that makeup encompasses. This aligning of themselves with the feminist denunciation of the pressure of the canons of beauty towards women, allows them to show themselves as beautiful as they are in a natural, free, self-chosen light.

According to Diana Cabral, who, in her Ph.D. thesis provides a comprehensive analysis of *Chicana* fashion, "we lack awareness of many more unique *Chicana* experiences revolving around clothing and fashion and how those experiences and the clothing/fashion play a role in their lives and in the development of their identities" (1). However, and as stated in the introduction of this work, clothing implies communication and the transmission of a message (Barnard), and in the case of the women in the image in Figure 5.2, the role of both their clothes and attitude is clear. Moreover, I would add that the choice of these clothes and attitude, and especially of the body language in the very particular case of that image, is a completely conscious personal choice, and thus the communication that it provokes and the message it sends is also a consciously articulated one. The women in the picture, therefore, perform a conscious act of subversion through it, or, in other words, perform *subversion and deviation through the conscious*, and thus are seeking a very particular response on the part of those looking at them.

Difficult as it is to establish a general conjecture on the way *Chicana* activists in the Sixties and Seventies dressed and on how they used their clothes and bodies to express and perform the revolution they were struggling for, I would at this point highlight the relevance of the indigenous elements in the form of clothes or ornaments for the women (and men) who were active during the *Movimiento*, and particularly during the feminist one. According to Cabral, "*Chicanas* are mestizos who honor and respect their indigenous lineage. Since the *Chicano* movement, a reclaiming of indigenous ancestry has continued to evolve in *Chicana* identity" (12). The idea of the vindication of the indigenous heritage of *Chicanos* and their representation of their multiply colonized, and thus culturally rich and complex cultural, social and linguistic heritage, was a core issue in the *Chicano* nationalist discourse, first, and in the *Chicana* feminist one later. The groundbreaking work by Gloria Anzaldúa, *Borderlands. La Frontera. The New Mestiza* (1987), clearly articulated the multicultural and multilayered essence of the *mestiza* woman, of her ethnic and cultural heritage, diversity and complexity, as well as the several forms in which discrimination and subjugation had been exerted upon these women. It seems, therefore, natural that at a time when there was a demand for the recognition of a silenced indigenous past, indigenous symbols were shown up in the clothing, the use of language and, in general, in the several acts and public demonstrations that members of the *Chicano* movement performed, and in those of women, particularly. These, and especially the indigenous clothes and ornaments that, in particular, *Chicana* activists showed in public, became symbols and conveyers of a clear and loud vindication of their ethnic past, heritage and, ultimately, pride. Moreover, this move towards the recovery of indigenous symbols was also performed by the participants in the hippie movement who very often looked at Native American traditions in their looks and customs. The spiritual connection of the Native American communities with the land was regarded as an extremely appealing vital attitude for hippies, whose search for Arcadia and a natural free relationship with the earth was symbolized in Native American thought and spirituality.

Several visual accounts of the moment show women (and men) wearing plain, white t-shirts with an Aztec eagle on them, or carrying banners with the same image. The eagle, symbol of the United Farm Workers, identifies and aligns them, on the one hand, with said movement and its struggle (the defense of the *braceros'* rights and the denunciation of their harsh living and working situation), but also connects them to their indigenous heritage and defines them ethnically within the North American socioethnic intricate and complex reality.

The ultimate symbol, however, of women's participation in La Causa in general, and in the farmers' struggle in particular, is Dolores Huerta, marching with César Chávez in Figure 5.1, who became an essential figure of the *Chicanos'* plight. The multiple and diverse photographic representations of the *Chicana* leader throughout her most active years always portray an active, voiced woman, and thus the symbol of the acquisition of a voice and agency on the part of women. Her manners depict a strong woman and her look, in very general terms, is humble and plain, like that of those she is striking for. In the many photographs that have been published, Dolores Huerta is always accompanied by the symbols that characterize the UFW, in the form of a banner or when she uses her body to convey a political message, through wearing a t-shirt with a clear political message, as one which reads "There's blood on those grapes! Don't buy Gallo Wine." In this particular case, the t-shirt calls for a boycott on grapes and wine, as a tool of denunciation

Figure 5.1 Dolores Huerta and César Chávez walk with picket sign
Courtesy of LA Public Library. Shades of LA Collection

and a demand for change in the terrible working conditions that the *braceros* who harvested them had to endure (harsh living conditions, indiscriminate use of pesticides, low wages, illegality, etc.). In this way, Dolores Huerta, like many other activists, became a political symbol and her body a conveyor of a political message. Once again, the lack of external ornamentations, definite hairstyle or makeup proves that Huerta and other activists were committed women, whose agency and power came from their political ideas and will to be active, rather than from the way they looked, as demanded by the pressure of societal roles on gender, and particularly on women.

Similarly, the struggle of Huerta and her peers, as well as that of *Chicano/a* activists in general, vindicated the indigenous heritage of both urban *Chicanos* and farm workers. In many of her appearances, as we saw with the case of the female Brown Berets, Huerta wore the traditional indigenous poncho, a huipil, where the Aztec eagle symbolic of the UFW and its strikes was inscribed. Thus, tradition and contemporaneity became part of the struggle of the *Movimiento*, and of the *Chicanas* too. The choice of an indigenous element, as proved before, became a clear political act, and like all the actions of the UFW in particular, Huerta's was a clear move towards subversion through the conscious, and in this case through the loud voice, the clear acts and a very particular, self-conscious look and attitude.

However, when looking at and analyzing many of the numerous pictures that were taken and publicized during the *Movimiento*, and in particular in marches and demonstrations such as the *Chicano Moratorium*, I arrive at two clear conclusions: on the one hand, that the majority of the people involved in these demonstrations and public actions were male, and on the other, that when women are seen as actively participating in the marches and the diverse political actions, very often I can see that their external look is neutral and shows no hint of ethnic identification, or even subversion of the codes of dress of the times. This is the case with the women in the following photographs, whose clothing adheres essentially to the mainstream fashion of the Sixties for women, and thus no rebellion is communicated through their look.

Figures 5.2 and 5.3 are shots of political actions organized by different factions of the *Chicano* movement, a protest action in front of a Marine Corps' recruiting station and a shot of the *Chicano Moratorium* of 1970. All of them show the small number of women involved in the actions, in contrast to the majority of men present in them. The women in the pictures, moreover, appear to be conforming to the aesthetic and fashion mores of the Sixties and Seventies, and their clothes and hairstyles comply with the norms. However, these women are undoubtedly rebellious and voiced women who adhere to *La Causa* and take the step of 'going out into the streets' and protesting for what they think is a just cause. As will be suggested in this general analysis of the use of individual external appearance by *Chicanas* in the Sixties and Seventies, we can infer that when women possess a very clear, loud and articulated political discourse and agenda, their external appearance plays a secondary role in the set of tools that are utilized to socially and publicly take part in such a struggle. In this case, the body (the female body

Figure 5.2 Chicano Moratorium Committee antiwar demonstrators
Courtesy of *Los Angeles Times* Photographic Archive, Library Special Collections, Charles E. Young Research Library, UCLA

Figure 5.3 Chicano Moratorium Committee antiwar demonstrators
Courtesy of *Los Angeles Times* Photographic Archive, Library Special Collections, Charles E. Young Research Library, UCLA

in particular) does not necessarily become a vehicle of transmission of political values and a certain subversive attitude towards the mandates of society, as this role is performed through the public enunciation of a clear political message, by means of diverse political actions. The body, as an essential element of a person's individual agency, in sum, is not a tool of protest, but a site of protest, *per se*.

In other cases, the women who are represented in the photographs are very generally dressed in the casual, natural modes of the Sixties, but with a slight reminiscence of the hippie, subversive for many, fashion of the times. These women wore pants as their everyday look (mostly jeans) and presented themselves with clean faces, devoid of any kind of makeup or special ornamentation.

In different visual representations taken during protest action within *La Marcha de la Reconquista* in the year 1971, we observe once again the unbalanced number of male and female members of the *Movimiento* who generally took part in the demonstrations and marches. It is interesting to note that in most of the photographs of the time, women are at the front of said demonstrations as fully active in them, carrying the banners and thus representing *La Causa*. However, in some instances, the banners use the word *Chicano* (solely in its masculine form) to express the fight of the community. The lack of the feminine form in the term is proof of the above-mentioned patriarchal ideology within the Movement, as well as of the predominance of men (and male vindications) over women in the first stages of the *Chicano* struggle. Observing some of these photographs, I come to the conclusion that many of women who appear in them as active members of the demonstrations, align themselves with the juvenile, hippie-like fashion of the time, where women wore jeans (shorts, long pants, and overalls) and in many cases, plain t-shirts with no political message conveyed on them. In most of the cases, too, the women have either plain ponytails or unsophisticated haircuts. Similarly, they wear no makeup or ornamentation. In sum, a simple glance at some of the various photographs of the time show that the women in these demonstrations, *Chicana* activists and politically conscious women, do not express any kind of contestation or subversion through their physical look, and more specifically through the hyperfeminization of their look, but they adopt the common one that the juvenile revolution provoked by the hippie movement brought with it during the decades of the struggles for civil rights. Very probably, and among the *Chicano* community, these women provoked a certain mistrust as they were defying the status quo of their community – in this case, not because they had joined the *Movimiento*, but because of their agentic, voiced and powerful attitude. What made these women, and all the activists of the Sixties and Seventies, subversive and contestatory was definitely their empowerment and their search for a public voice and a visible, recognized-by-all identity. Their first-line appearance in the *Movimiento* and their obviously protagonistic position within demonstrations, as can be observed in many photographs of the period, give these women a certain subversive identity that they consciously achieve through their attitude and commitment to *La Causa*.

Interestingly enough, and when it comes to describing the use of clothing and personal ornamentation as a means of communication, and in this particular case a message of subversion, rebellion and, in sum, disidentification with the general state of affairs, the men in some of the photographs of the time lead us to much more interesting conclusions. First, they almost always outnumber the women in the photographs, and thus, in the demonstrations. Second, they are all obviously young men who are active participants in the *Chicano* movement and their commitment to it is very probably unquestionable. However, it is extremely interesting to see that most of them use their body language and particularly their attire in a nonstandard way and they adhere to the hippie mores and fashions of the time: long hair, bandanas holding it to their foreheads, beards and sometimes, bare chests. This free, public display of the male body proves, on the one hand, that the *Movimiento Chicano*, as well as others, was very much influenced by the hippie ideology of the search for spiritual and physical freedom. The liberation from the strict codes of decency and morality that traditional Western clothing norms and rules represented was, in fact, one of the signs of identification of the hippie movement. This was understood as an affront to normative tradition, both Anglo and Mexican, as Rorabaugh explains when describing the reaction of middle-class parents to their sons' looks and behavior:

> To the older generation, this male garb was unsettling on several levels. The rejection of traditional mainstream dress was almost total. For middle-class parents, the failure of sons to wear starched white shirts and ties, even for such formal events as hippie weddings, meant that sons were rejecting the idea of being middle class. (. . .) This was precisely what hippies intended. The wearing of blue jeans upset parents, because jeans were identified with farmers, the working class, and the poor. By insisting on tight jeans, youth were engaging in a sexual display that challenged the middle-class view that respectability required loose-fitting clothes. Hippie dress challenged orthodoxy on every level.
>
> (103)

And it challenged Mexican orthodoxy too, as it challenged the gender roles and expectations of the community. Moreover, the lenient and untroubled presentation of the uncovered male body reveals the markedly patriarchal spirit and essence of the *Movimiento* where there were differing moral standards for men and women.

There are, similarly, visual accounts which show a clearer identification of women activists with the probably more sophisticated hippie fashion that was popular during the civil rights movements. In them, the women align themselves with this look, and can thus also be considered to be performing a subversive act through this identification with the rebellious, irreverent, hippie fashion. These 'hippie-looking, *Chicana*' women represent, in my view, a double kind of subversion or degree of rebellion: physical and attitudinal. The adoption of hippie symbols such as the long hair and the bandana holding it firstly connects them to the hippie cause, which, as stated before, looked at Native American customs, traditions and, in this case, bodily ornamentation as a source of inspiration. In the case of *Chicana* activists, the use of the lace on their foreheads connects them, as mentioned before, to their specific indigenous past, and thus supports physically and visually one of the causes of the *Chicano* movement (and the *Chicana* feminist one). Similarly, their plain, clean faces devoid of makeup situate them in the fashion trends of the civil rights movement where human beauty was to be demonstrated simply and naturally (and particularly that of females, which had always been conditioned by the mandates of beauty standards). Finally, it is their public presentation and attitude, as voiced, politically conscious and active women that make them fully rebellious and subversive. Many of the visual accounts of the marches and demonstrations depict them as revolutionary, strong, committed women, unafraid of marching for a just cause. Finally, children are present in the many of the accounts of the marches too, a fact which becomes central and essential, fully contradicting the idea that *Chicano* male activists had that the female cause and the feminist vindications were a tool to dismantle the traditional familial structure of the community, the backbone of the group and the only conveyor and guarantee of its perpetuation.

To conclude this chapter devoted to drawing some general observations on the utilization of physical appearance and bodily attitude by voiced *Chicana* activists, I can affirm that what most clearly depicts these women is their very conscious political discourse, which they exhibited through an active participation in political marches, demonstrations or other kinds of actions. In most cases, and in contrast to the situation of the women of the Forties that have been looked at previously, these women do not 'make use' of a clearly subversive, defiant look to confront the gender and social norms imposed on them, but they use their voices and articulated political and ideological messages to do so. In most cases, except for in the case of the female Brown Berets, who had to adapt to a very clear and unbreakable code of military behavior and physical look through the use of a uniform, the *Chicana* activists show very little bodily ornamentation, unsophisticated, nongender-marked attire, no makeup and very plain hairstyles. This style adheres to the hippie and feminist mores of the Sixties, where a connection to the body in a natural, unsophisticated way was mostly preferred and valued. Similarly, the feminist movement understood that the use of makeup and other mandates related to the established canon of beauty imposed upon women through the ages (including body weight) had to be strongly rejected and women had to be free to choose the way they wanted to look and be looked at. In the case of the farmer union activist Dolores Huerta, among others, her ideological struggle was reinforced by her clear identification with an indigenous heritage and the defense of the people who worked the lands, who often had a strong indigenous heritage and ethnic component. In this case, she and other women activists of the times opted to include in their clothes elements that had a clear indigenous essence, thereby making their public, physical look a conveyor of an ethnic identification mark, and thus political. This is the case with the woman at the back and in the center of Figure 5.4, whose poncho identifies her both with the *Chicana* indigenous heritage and the hippie movement, which looked at the native traditions for spiritual and creative inspiration.

Figure 5.4 Chicano Moratorium Committee demonstrators picket the San Fernando Police

Courtesy of *Los Angeles Times* Photographic Archive, Library Special Collections, Charles E. Young Research Library, UCLA

In all cases, the women who were active in both the *Chicano* and the *Chicana* feminist movements were politically conscious individuals, who sought a voice and an active role both within the mainstream society and the *Chicano* community, and they performed *subversion and deviation through the conscious*, and used all the tools in their hands to perform said subversion: their voices, their ideology and political agenda, and finally their bodies and attitude, which no longer showed submission to, and/or acceptance of, what had been chosen and imposed upon them. These women showed no need for the articulation and exposure of a rebellious, defiant, exaggerated, hyperfeminized image through clothes, hairstyles and/or makeup. Their bodies were no longer tools of protest, but sites of protest *per se*.

Chapter 6

Cholas
Adapting to other norms in the Nineties

6.1. Life and expectations for US young women in the Nineties

In Patrick J. Kiger's words, when we think of the Nineties, in contrast to previous decades, he admits that they

> elude such facile characterization. It was a decade of jarring, sometimes incongruous motifs without a theme to tie them coherently together – (. . .) Indeed, the last 10 years of the 20th century was a decade with an existential crisis of sorts, more of a vague borderline than a pivotal moment. (. . .) Similarly, the 1990s was a time in which the foundation was laid for the startling, disruptive changes that would suddenly emerge in the early 21st century. (. . .) It also was a decade which saw the ripening and blossoming of changes that started earlier – from the rise of the Internet and wireless mobile communication to the shift from an analog to a digital information culture, to the shift to economic globalization, in which investment and finance reached across borders and manufacturing flowed to developing countries with the cheapest labor.
>
> (n.p.)

Regardless of the idea of transition and indefinition exhibited in the above words, the Nineties in the United States were a time of great economic prosperity, cultural expansion and technological boom. The civil rights movement and the feminist revolution had, at least on the surface, brought radical changes to the country, and the ideal of democracy and equality was, at least theoretically, a reality for the Nineties young generation, offspring of the revolution.

In economic terms, the country was doing better than ever before, with an evident fall in unemployment rates and the Soviet Union no longer being a threat to the international stability of capitalism, and in the country, it was a time of multiculturalism and diversity. Similarly, women entered the workforce and young girls attended university. Television and cinema boomed and became goods of mass consumption, communication systems started to change from analog to digital versions, globalization was starting to exist as an international system of transnational political and cultural relationships, and the World Wide Web would forever change the way we understand the world in general and life in particular.

But if there is a term that best defines the clear lack of definition and blurring of social categories, especially for the youth, that occurred in the Nineties (as opposed to that of the previous generations) it is that of "Generation X." Named after a novel by Douglas Coupland published in the year 1991 (although the term had been coined by Robert Capa in the Fifties) (Ulrich 3), this generation accounts for a whole demographic one rather than a particular subcultural one. The grunge music and style that predominated in the Nineties could be considered both subcultural and mainstream at the same time, because of its nihilistic and nonconformist essence on the one hand, and as a consequence of its massive consumption and existence in the mainstream music and fashion industries. This continuous contradiction is what marked the spirit of the generation and their philosophy. In John Ulrich's words, "the term 'Generation X' marks precisely this paradoxical borderline status (inside and outside, within and against the mainstream). (. . .) Here subcultural identity is dependent on its differential relation to the mainstream, and subcultural signifying practices are themselves routinely appropriated by the 'accelerated,' dominant culture, and thus 'sold out' before their time" (19). The members of the generation thus lived "in a culture where 'true' resistance and rebellion are said to be impossible because they are always already co-opted, where no 'authentic' individual identity can be expressed, because it is always already mediated through commodities" (20).

The young girls of the Nineties (and the Eighties) undoubtedly had better opportunities than their forebears and the attendance rates at university or at higher education institutions and thus working opportunities were much better than those of the previous generations. From a 21st century European perspective, however, it is interesting to note that many of the definitions of the Generation X, which, as Ulrich points at, include a demographic generation rather than a particular subcultural piece of said generation, leave aside the social, economic and educational realities of members of that same generation who lived in the margins of the same dominant culture that commodified the former. For the particular focus of this volume, the definitions leave aside the young generation of Mexican Americans who existed outside the realms of mainstream culture and mainstream personal opportunities. Many of these, as will be explained in the following pages, had very few educational and personal possibilities and their inevitable destinies would always occur in the peripheral areas of US cities, in *barrios* and ghettos. With very few opportunities to leave these deprived areas of the cities, and not being accounted for by the general mainstream discourse that was prevalent in the Nineties, nor by the economic opportunities that the wealthy and prosperous generation brought with it, these groups found a way out in organized gangs or *clickas*, which offered them an opportunity to improve their economic status, on the one hand, and provided them with a sense of belonging that the mainstream society denied them. Needless to say, not all young boys and girls from the *barrios* joined gangs, just as not all middle-class boys and girls followed the grunge style and nihilistic attitude towards life. However, for the purpose of this work, it is my intention to look at the way in which gang style and attitude was influential in the US Nineties *barrios*. Young girls who adhered to this style demonstrated their subcultural, subversive identity through their personal style and attitude, and it is my aim to draw comparative conclusions with regards to the other two groups of women I have included before: *Pachucas* and *Chicanas*.

6.2. Women's fashion in the Nineties

As explained previously, the Nineties were a transitional decade, in which most of the big possibilities achieved by the previous generations were assimilated as natural (such as the rights of women and other minorities), and similarly, many of the great revolutions (such as the technological one) that would became a reality at the beginning of the 21st century started to develop. The young people of the Nineties thus became young in a situation where the fight for their personal rights was not supposedly as necessary as it had been for the previous generations. Therefore, they grew up believing that they belonged to a group that differed widely both culturally and in terms of social and moral values from their predecessors. Additionally, their access to goods and their full immersion in the capitalist consumerist system had shaped their understanding of both themselves and of society as a whole.

In terms of fashion and their relationship with clothes, body adornment and, in sum, their public representation, these young people, as a target group of the fashion industry, had a wider variety of styles, brands, and role models to choose from. The fashion industry no longer marked the look and style of the majority as a unitary group, as there was already a great heterogeneity and variety in styles and looks. Therefore, in contrast to the more restrictive fashion and style choices of the previous generations, in the Nineties there were already a large number of subcultural (or nonconforming to the mainstream fashion rule) groups and styles that young people could align with. However, as stated before, the grunge style and attitude was prevalent and relevant among the US young generation of the Nineties. This consisted mostly of a laid-back, casual, consciously scruffy style, where both boys and girls adopted similar looks and the gender markers were not so obviously indicated by clothing and general physical look. Young girls who adopted a clearly grunge style depicted a gender-neutral look: big, baggy pants, plaid shirts, long, uncombed hair. As will be seen later, though, there are some elements of this style that coincide with those of *Cholas* who adopt a 'tomboy' look, devoid of a feminine mark. The long, natural hair, the big Pendleton shirts, baggy jeans and t-shirts are reminiscent of the *Chola* style. However, in the case of the latter, these exaggerate their femininity (and their more aggressive attitude) through a very marked lip and eye makeup, and in many cases, with more elaborate hairstyles, as will be seen in the following pages.

Regardless of the obvious impact that grunge music, style and life attitude had on many young people of the Nineties United States, and because of the greater heterogeneity and choice that the young generation had, the idea that clothing and style may communicate rebellion or subversion was not as evident as the previous generations had experienced. Followers of the grunge style evidently expressed their dissatisfaction towards life and a sense of alienation from a consumerist culture that had metaphorically swallowed them and in which they actively participated. In the particular case of young girls, they very soon became the targets of a fierce consumerist system, which exposed them continuously to messages regarding femininity and beauty. These messages, as in the fashion system, which in the last two decades of the 20th century were endlessly reproduced on television and channels such as MTV, were, as a rule, patriarchal and capitalist (Guy, Green and Banim 6) and reproduced a beauty myth (Wolf) that was constraining and based on an idealized, oversexualized representation of womanhood, and was constructed for a patriarchal masculine gaze. In this context, where visual representations of femininity and masculinity, of beauty and success were incessantly available to the young generation, and in fact became the mark of a generation, clothing and style became an essential tool for group identification (but not necessarily a subversive one). In fact,

> for young women, style gives meaning, validation and coherence to their group identity – it defines who is part of the group and who is external to the group. It is a visible expression of the individual belonging to a group. Clothing is part of tribalism and of social status and, in that sense, can be seen as opposed to individuality. The group recognizes itself and is recognized by others. It can also be related to hostility and conflict, defining those who are members and those who are not and constructing one's identity within conflicting groups.
>
> (Guy, Green and Banim 29)

These last ideas apply clearly to Mexican American young girls of the Nineties, the focus of this study, those who adopt the *Chola* style. In their particular case, the idea of belonging and identifying in opposite ways is very group-specific. Young women and men from the US *barrios* were also part of the above-mentioned capitalist and patriarchal system of consumerism, but in their case, a difficult sociocultural and educational situation adds to the idea of belonging to one group, and thus not belonging to another one. The educational opportunities for these young men and women were obviously fewer and more complicated than those of the mainstream, better-off young groups of the dominating classes and ethnic groups. Thus, some of these young *Chicanos*, relegated as they were from the mainstream cultural and social everyday life, created their own set of cultural and social rules, which they identified with through clothing and style, among other devices. Similarly to what has been described before, these style codes aligned them with certain groups from their own community and concomitantly disassociated them from others, such as their traditional community and the mainstream one. Their clothing and style, therefore, connected them to a group, and in most cases communicated and expressed an angry rebellion towards a system that left them aside.

6.3. Gangs and *Cholo/a* style in 20th century *barrios*

Before delving into the following chapter, I assume it necessary to clarify that this study does not pretend to connect all girls from the *barrios* with the gang system. However, it acknowledges the fact that the effect of the gangs, both on the personal lives and the styles of these girls, was obvious. Therefore, regardless of the fact that they were involved in the gang system, or lived around it, many of these girls adopted a gang-related *Chola* style, which will be the focus of this study.

In her groundbreaking work *Going Down to the Barrio*, Joan W. Moore studied the evolution of two gangs in East Los Angeles from the Fifties until the Seventies. The study grounded some theoretical assumptions about how to understand the creation and existence of gangs, and about the way their members become affiliated and function inside the gang system. She points out that sociologists like James Short first defined the gangs, not because of their degree of delinquency or criminality, but within the normal processes of deviance that occur during adolescence (1990). What is also true, Moore states, is that at some point, gangs evolve into two possible scenarios. The first is what she calls "the resistance theory" scenario, and addresses the fact that "gangs are potentially revolutionary organizations of youth that give voice to the frustrations of oppressed minorities"; they are "'oppositional' because they do and say things that challenge and flout conventional authority" (Moore 42). However, for Moore, the gangs are defiant and resistant, but not revolutionary. The next scenario, the scholar adds, which contrasts with the previous one is what she calls "the Illicit Opportunity Scenario," which defends the postulate that "gangs evolve into criminal organizations, in which the adolescent cohorts serve as recruiting and training grounds for criminal enterprises" (42). The scholar then discusses the different sources of this criminalization, as well as the position of diverse researchers on this subject, stating finally that the gangs of East Los Angeles evolved between the Fifties and Seventies, but not into criminal organizations. She states that the general evolution of gangs led them into increased deviance, because of the ever-harder life situation of their members, especially of those who had been incarcerated, and because of the recurrent need to control them with diverse programs or police and even media harassment. The scholar argues that the more deviant the group becomes, the more extensive in terms of ages and rituals the recruitment process becomes. In her study, Moore states that the degree of violence and the means of this violence had increased among the gangs she studied, the use of drugs had increased too, the general view of gangs had become more negative in general terms, and finally, the gender control of women was more prevalent in all groups. In sum, the gangs had not evolved into criminal organizations but had definitely become more deviant and inertly aggressive.

In the last few decades of the 20th century and at the beginning of the 21st, *Chicano* sociologist James Diego Vigil contributed widely to the study of gangs among *Chicano* youngsters. Among the reasons given by the scholar to explain the affiliation of young kids with the gang subculture, Vigil says that the complexity of their socioeconomic and cultural situation can be described as "multiple marginality." This notion encompasses the varied array of causes that keep the boys in the *barrios* in a situation that takes them far away from wealth and power.

When Vigil outlines the several socioeconomic reasons that have favored the prolific emergence of Mexican American gangs in the Los Angeles area, he refers to the "continuous immigration of Mexicans into Southern California and the problems these immigrants face in adjusting to urban society, especially their marginalization within it, which also affects later generations" (*Rainbow* 31). He states that during the massive floods of new settlers into the city, both Anglos and Mexicans, the urbanization processes that the city went through occurred mainly in the hands of the Anglo settlers, who built to the south and west of the city. The *pueblo* that was once the Mexican part of the city became a segregated, isolated *barrio*. Similarly, the new Mexican population, poorer than California Mexicans, settled to the east of the city, close to their workplaces and where rents were lower (and conditions worse). These *barrios* are still, today, "distanced from whites, rundown in appearance, and subject to the usual marginalization experiences that generate street gangs" (*Rainbow* 35). The ecological environment of these *barrios* is generally degraded, and freeways, roads, bridges, etc. are part of a landscape that affects the general psychology of the 'hoods. Most of the younger dwellers of these *barrios* experience prejudice at school, which in many cases, according to the scholar, leads to high numbers of school dropouts. Comparing mainstream Los Angeles with the Pico Gardens *barrio*, as an example, he says: "[T]here are ecological contrasts (visual and spatial distinctions), economic strains (underclass and secondary labor market), social dysfunctions (family stress and school failure), cultural discontinuities (hybrid mixture, syncretic cholo), and psychological ordeals (adolescent status crisis and group identity)" (*Projects* 57). In his understanding, and as a result, the kids spend most of their time out in the street, socializing and adopting the street values and norms. For him, "when street socialization replaces socialization by conventional caretakers, it becomes a key factor in developing not only different social bonds but different aspirations for achievement, levels and intensities of participation, and belief patterns" (Vigil, *Rainbow* 22). These problems, such as "language problems, cultural and ethnic identity conflict, general malaise and discrimination (. . .) generally precede and contribute to involvement in the gang" (*Rainbow* 41). This situation, and a generally difficult family situation (poverty, absence of a father figure in many cases), as well as a strong social control by police and other institutions, lead many of these kids into becoming a *Cholo*.

Vigil explains that the origin of the word "dates from the Spanish colonial period, when it meant 'mestizo'" (*Rainbow* 44). Today, it implies living on the margins. For the scholar, *choloization* is a syncretic process that encompasses the mixture of cultures into a new subculture and results "in a variety of characteristics that reflect the *Chicano* gang subculture in terms of organization, structure, values and norms, and social and cultural habits" (*Rainbow* 44). This applies also to *Cholas*. However, these are faced with a stronger kind of discrimination on the part of their peers due to the obvious gender-based hierarchy the gang is organized into.

This street socialization process and acquisition of street values and norms often encourage the young dwellers of the *barrio* to get involved in the gang system directly, and other times to just support it. In this context, jumping into the gang is, for some, an elaborate ritual, and in some other cases, just a simple 'two-punch' issue that takes them into the gang in a natural, nonplanned way. However, prior to this, the young kids take part in small thefts and walks around the *barrio* and others to encounter rival gangs, including at school (Vigil 1988, 2002, 2007, 2008). In the case of kids who drop out of school (who are numerous in the case of the less privileged *barrios*), the amalgamation of the social conditions of the *barrio*, the slow but effective socialization process they go through and the psychological characteristics of the transition time in adolescence leads them into joining the gang (Vigil *Projects*).

Once inside it, the gang represents a set of norms and conduct, as well as values that every member of it chooses to respect and defend. The gang becomes *la familia* and members of it have to remain loyal and respectful towards it. Keeping one's word and sharing with other members are key values in the system, as well as paying respect to the older members of the group, the *veteranos*. As a means of dealing with fear and danger, the members of the gang are required to demonstrate a certain state of mind, a *locura*, which, in Vigil's words, is a "state of mind in which various quasi-controlled actions denoting a type of craziness or wildness occur, giving the appearance of a lack of impulse control" (*Rainbow* 63). This state displays "a destructive fearlessness, toughness, daring and other unpredictable forms of behavior" (*Rainbow* 63). All in all, the state of *locura* comprises, in general terms, a high degree of violence and ruthlessness when defending one's turf (territory) and values.

6.3.1. The girls in/around the gang system: Cholas

It is a fact that girls have always been part of the gang system, either as companions or as active members of gangs. Jody Miller, in *The Girls in the Gang: What We've Learned from Two Decades of Research*, provides a thorough review of the literature related to female gang activity, which, she says, is scarcer than that about similar male activity. The scholar states that female gang affiliation data show that girls are less involved in gang activity. This can be related, among other reasons, to the fact that often girls are involved in gangs for a shorter period of time than boys and in many cases do not participate as much in the most violent activities of the group (178). The reason for the girls joining these gangs are manifold, or in sum, as Vigil calls it, the main general reason is "multiple marginality," which stems from the economic, educational, class, ethnic and familiar situations of the girls, as well as from their general position in the overall arrangement of society. Among these all-encompassing, holistic sources of multiple marginalization, Miller highlights the way different studies (Campbell 1984; Moore 1991; Portillos 1999) have considered the family to be one of the sources for joining the gang (182) – sometimes as a way to escape abuse, violence, and other negative factors, or because the family was directly involved in the gang system, and at other times to avoid "oppressive patriarchal conditions in the home" (182).

Once the girls enter the gang, according to Miller, among other issues, they transgress the gender roles that are expected from them, and thus face what the scholar calls "social sanctions" (190) within and outside the gang. Entering the gang implies a strong gender deviation in the eyes of both mainstream society and those of their group, but if they take this deviance too far, they can also be sanctioned by other members of the gang, who may accuse them of not behaving appropriately in terms of sexuality, motherhood, drug use and/or violence. The girls, therefore, live in a continuous state of having to deal with a clear double standard when it comes to deciding the extent to which they have to deviate from the norm, as a consequence of the clear gender-based hierarchization of the gang system.

Although fewer girls than boys participate actively in the gang system, and consequently there are fewer studies about female gang participation than that of boys, according to Vigil, there has been a growth in the activity of girls in gangs (2007). According to the scholar and field researcher, different factors may have contributed to this shift and one of them has to do with acculturation patterns that have occurred among *Latino/Chicano* communities. The transformation of traditional *Marianismo* and the female cultural role that relegated women to the homes and thus kept them away from street socialization processes is changing and women are more 'out' than before, and thus more subject to gang involvement. On the other hand, there are more girls who have been raised in a gang environment, and thus the chances of them getting involved in gang style and culture are greater. According to the scholar, there are three kinds of female gangs: autonomous ones, gangs that depend on a male one and finally mixed-gender ones. In general terms, many of the female gangs depend on a male one, and in many cases the girls involved in them are either girlfriends or sisters of boys in the male *clicka*.

Vigil points out that the reasons for girls to get involved in gang activity are the same as those for boys, mainly arising from the multiple marginalization pattern: "poverty and isolation within many *barrios*, poor educational systems that do not address the needs of minority youth, and familial problems combined with the fixture of the street gang as socialization agent. (...) Many join the gang for support and friendship, particularly when such support is unavailable in the family" (*Projects* 110). Girls, who suffer not only this multiple marginalization, but on top of that, that of gender, and are undervalued by society and their own male peers, join the gang as a symbol of "a tangible break from traditional cultural values of men and women" (*Projects* 111). This move, for girls, implies a highly deviant attitude in the eyes of the community, but for them, it is a way of gaining respect, of being "someone" (*Projects* 115). Many of them come from difficult family situations, where drug or alcohol abuse may occur, the scholar points out, and some of them have been the victims of sexual abuse (within the family in many cases). For them, joining the gang is a way of gaining empowerment, emotional support and self-esteem (*Projects* 114–15). Some others come from families that are already part of the gang system and joining the gang seems a natural life move for them. Although Vigil defends the idea that most of the *barrio* girls do not get involved and keep up with the community's tradition, he also expresses the notion that the social pressure and expectations they are exposed to in a way push them into inevitably joining it. He says:

> However, for a minority of girls who do become involved in street life, traditional values actually work against them, helping distance them from cultural moorings. They are labeled because of their street involvement, suggestive clothing, makeup and hairstyle choices which reflect a "street style" and, as a result, are susceptible to becoming socially isolated. Traditional values protect most young women, but decreasingly so for girls from "*cholo*" families. These girls bear the *chola* label in a deeply personalized, stigmatizing manner even before their involvement in the deviant subculture. Thus, social sanctions may be exacted on them early on and some may not have the individual fortitude or social opportunities necessary for them to recover. Pushed into this role some become active as a matter of course. Since they are already socially isolated with the unshakable label of deviant, they rationalize fulfilling these lowered expectations, by simply joining the gang.
>
> ("Female Gangs" 55)

Taking into account the strong traditional gender roles perpetuated in and by the gang system, in many cases the girls who abandon their families to join the gang encounter the same kind of gender expectations within the group. The male and female roles that are prominent within the gang support a very traditional, dominant, violent understanding of machismo, and for a boy in the gang to be a man, he has to know how to 'keep his lady in check.' The girls are required to be submissive and accept their roles as sexual objects, and "to make the needs of her family and husband her first priority" (Vigil *Projects* 116). Boys, according to Vigil, prefer 'good girls' who stay at home rather than 'bad girls' who are sexually active. A girl's respect and power position, accordingly, depends on the boy she is with and her loyalty to him. The concept of girls as mere sexual objects is an everyday life issue in the gangs, and the girls accept this role to be accepted in the group, just as they accept being abused physically and verbally. According to Vigil, "female submission to this type of treatment is evidence of the self-destructive nature of gang activity. Interactions between males and females are, in a sense, a twisted enactment of the extremes of cultural gender-role definitions:

male dominance and female submissiveness" (*Projects* 119). In this context, teen pregnancies are highly common among gang members. In a study carried out by Anne Campbell in 1990, she pointed out that 94 percent of the girls involved in gangs became pregnant while they were associated with the gang (in Vigil *Rainbow*). This high pregnancy rate is a result, on the one hand, of the aforementioned gender roles. A man proves his love to his girl if he wants her to have his baby, and the girls understand that getting pregnant is a proof of love and respect. In many cases, as Vigil points out, the members of the gang choose to be parents at a very early age because they have assimilated the fact that their life will be short.

In this very particular socioeconomic, cultural and personal context, it is the aim of the following pages to examine the way in which these women defy the existing normative agenda (both of their own community and of the mainstream one) through their attire and attitude. In Enrique C. Orozco's words, in a description of *Cholo/a* attitude at schools during the late Nineties,

> [p]resently, among the biosocially arrested personalities, crude and monosyllabic English, pidgin English or Spanish, and an abrasive and hostile demeanor characteristically persist. So does the "mad-dogging" posture technique of intimidation. The dress mode had changed by the 1980s in most urban centers, and by the 1990s the traditional garb among many had been discarded. Consequently, it has become more trendy and spiffy. Black caps, shaved heads and black jackets have also become more popular.
>
> The so-called *Cholas*, cha cha girls, or *locas* are the female counterparts to the *batos*. They are as demoralized and as socio-psychologically alienated as their male counterparts. Many continue to wear cosmetics with the traditional semi-raccoon exotic mask look, and the "drugstore spiked blond or redheaded look". (. . .) The object of their distinctively defiant dress modes and demeanor is to brashly set themselves apart from other students. These rough and tough self-images are socially negative as they are intended to offend.
>
> (65–6)

6.4. The *Chola* style politics

As stated in the previous section of this volume, the gang or *clicka* represents a tight, hierarchically arranged system with a very strong and definite moral, behavioral and even style code. The gang members distinguish themselves from other groups, and adopt among themselves a clear style, a set of movements, postures and, in general, a body attitude that expresses their commitment to the group, as well as their sense of sharing and belonging. Thus, their clothes, their looks, their body gestures, their graffiti and, in sum, their style politics mark them as a particular gang's members and speak for themselves. In Susan Phillips's words, "graffiti are a crucial mechanism for the acts of representing through which gang members intertwine their emotional and political concerns" (117). Clothing and external appearance, and thus style, function likewise. This style, as will be observed in the following lines, influenced the stylistic choices of many of the young girls and boys in the US *barrios*, who, irrespective of their participation or not in the gang system, adopted its appearance and style. This applies to the young girls this chapter addresses. In it, I do not intend to judge or connect them to any group, but to look at the way they dress and the ideas they express through it.

According to Vigil, girls who affiliate with gangs or are related to them adopt a particular style, which describes them as gang-related girls even if they do not participate actively in them. The scholar points out the fact that the roles the girls take define their style. Thus, girls who adopt a tomboy attitude dress similarly to the boys, whereas the girls who adopt a more feminine role are dressed more provocatively. Most of the time, this style reinforces the sexual roles of boys and girls in the gang. The girls, who dress up to party wearing "very short spandex shorts" (Vigil *Projects* 121) and a little shirt, thus strengthen their sexual-object role, which the boys enjoy seeing and 'using,' but which these same boys reject when it comes to talking about how they would like their girlfriends to be and act. Exaggerated makeup, and especially eyeliner, also define *Chola* style, and as Mendoza-Denton pointed out in a study about this style, one girl said, "if you want to know who is a *Chola*, just look for the eyeliner. Everybody could notice that that's a chola" (55). Eyeliner, symbolic of a "war paint," is, for these girls, like the rest of their attire, a symbol of rejection of not only mainstream values, but also of the values and roles their parents may have taught them. Aligning themselves with this style, the girls in the gang express their total confrontation of a society that discriminates against them for several reasons and puts them in a state of multiple marginalization (Vigil *Projects*).

Lisa C. Dietrich points out, in her comprehensive portrayal of *Chicana* adolescents, that many of these girls adopt the gang style even before they join the gang (or even if they do not join it, I would add), marking themselves as 'gang-related' members. They generally adopt a style that is similar to that of their male peers and, according to the scholar,

> [t]hey wear large baggy pants or jeans, black flat shoes, and either t-shirts or long-sleeved Pendleton shirts. Their hair is worn long and straight, sometimes dyed an auburn color. When the girls "dress down," they spray their bangs straight up from their foreheads. The girls also wear very heavy makeup around their eyes and lips. They make what they called their "raccoon eyes" by outlining their eyes with black eyeliner and heavy mascara.
> (129)

This masculine style, says the scholar, represents a defiance towards the standard of femininity, as it "upsets notions of appropriate feminine behavior, distinguishing them from other *Chicanas*, as well as from their Asian, Anglo and African American counterparts" (129). However, I would add that there seems to be a contradiction in this overtly masculine style, as, on the other hand, their makeup seems to be exaggeratedly feminine. This makeup, no doubt, conveys a high degree of meaning and symbolism, because, as stated before, painting oneself is a symbolization of masking oneself. In this particular case, it is a war mask, as the girls are in a way stating that they are ready for war – war with the mainstream society, war with their parental traditions, war with their homeboys and even war with themselves. This overdone makeup, similarly, defies decency and morality, as traditionally in Western society this kind of exaggerated makeup has often been associated with prostitution. Very aggressive makeup has been considered, as occurs among animals, a symbol of sexual demand, a call for willingness.

As Marie "Keta" Miranda's interesting project with a group of gang girls demonstrates, the look Dietrich described in the Nineties was somehow prevalent some years later and in a different *barrio*. She describes the girls who took part in her project as follows:

> [M]ost of the girls wore dark red or burgundy lipstick; some outlined their lips with black eyeliner pencil. Their eye makeup was heavily applied; the most prevalent was black eyeliner and mascara. Some wore long ponytails, knotted at the very top of their heads, giving them more height, with long bangs arranged to fall over one eye. While a handful wore shorter hairstyles, bell-bottomed pants, ribbed tops covered by a net vest, and platform shoes, most wore red or black oversized baggy pants (called "Dickies"), large, loose t-shirts, and Hush Puppies, high-top tennis shoes, or Doc Marten copies.
>
> (27)

The homogeneity of the description is obvious and responds to the aforementioned need to belong and share that the girls (and boys) seek in the group. By dressing similarly, they not only adopt an individual attitude to the society they belong to, but a group attitude that makes them more powerful and thus, probably, aggressive. The clothing these girls adopt, although not aggressive in itself, hides the feminine body and leaves no room for femininity, and is accompanied by a more defiant facial language that depicts a provocative, rebellious body language and meaning. In Miranda's words, again, "the transgressive dress and style are both a derivative of and resistant to the gender order. An exaggeration of 'girl' through the pronouncement of lips and hair combines with an assertive use of clothing to hide the body" (82). Interestingly enough, too, the boys and girls in the gang seek uniformity and avoid any hint of individual identity, and clothes help them perform this group body language.

Having examined the conceptual and descriptive grounds of the way these women dress, I consider it interesting to look at how the women who were part of gangs or their lives evolving around them dressed in the Nineties. For this purpose, and bearing in mind that there is now much greater access to random pictures of *Cholas* and *Chicana* young girls due to the proliferation of visual material on the Web, the photographs that I observed to draw my interpretative conclusions are all representations of *barrio Chicana* young women of the Nineties, which are found in diverse open-access Web pages. These conclusions will be aimed at observing the relevance of communal heterogeneous dress as a code of belonging among young people who become part of what has been generally labeled as subcultural. However, and before delving more deeply into the matter, I believe it is necessary to clarify that there is no factual evidence of the fact that these women were active members of gang activity or were even related to it. What is common among all of them in the way they dressed and showed themselves in public is that they all adopted the *Chola* look, which, as we have seen, is clearly defined by the above words and descriptive annotations.

In many of the numerous photographs that can be found on the Web and in diverse social media (but which will not be reproduced for copyright and personal privacy issues), girls who are posing in front of the camera in different situations, some in the street, some others in more artificial settings, such as studios, or even inside homes, can be observed. Many of these girls adhere to what can be described as a *Chola* "femenine style" (Vigil). What is common to many of these photographs is that they are, most of the times, group photographs, where the girls are showing their friendship and camaraderie. In many of them, the girls pose demonstrating diverse attitudes towards the group, thereby communicating different identitarian and attitudinal poses and thus messages. These range from sweet smiles to defiant, grave, more aggressive looks. Most of these photographs definitely show pride and an energetic, strong pose and, consequently, identity. Generally, the girls' poses convey a clear sense of belonging and group identification, which is achieved by their very commonly homogeneous look and physical appearance. Their very mostly always long, dark, curly, backcombed hair, their markedly shaped eyebrows, their strongly painted lips, prove that their look and pose are aimed at communicating a clear sense of belonging both for themselves and the rest of the community. This look, style and attitude undoubtedly connects them to other *Cholas* or women of their *barrio*, probably with the same sociocultural background, thereby turning their bodies into labeling tools. These, on the one hand, identify them with a certain group and similarly disidentify them from others. On the other hand, this same look, makeup and hairstyle, together with the position and stance they adopt in many of the photographs, defines them as being concerned about their physical image and their beauty in general. They all conform to the beauty standards of their group. In many of the cases, the girls show themselves as women who expose their bodies freely and are dressed in a 'sexy' manner (taking into account the patriarchal standard of femininity and female desirability), and we can thus infer that they use and control them in the same manner. It is interesting to note, though, that the women activists I looked at in the previous chapter, who probably had a much more elaborate political discourse in terms of the female appropriation of the body, showed a more prudish general look, which also conformed in a more compliant way to the norms of moral codes that were prevalent in the Sixties and Seventies. These girls, in sum, may be described as what the standard rules of gender identification would define as 'feminine.' And I would add hyperfeminine, as they exaggerate traits and elements that have traditionally been regarded as marks of femininity and female sexuality (in terms of a patriarchal, masculine gaze), such as the lips and hair. In many cases, the photographs show that they overdo their traditionally considered feminine attributes by means of heavy makeup, an elaborate hairstyle, with conscious backcombing and subsequent expansion, and, in sum, a sexualization of their look (once again, taking into account masculine, patriarchal standards). In many cases, the girls wear very short tops that reaffirm their breasts and exposes them, reproducing a masculine female sexual imaginary and placing themselves as objects of male desire. However, starting from the premise that girls in the Nineties performed their gender and ethnic identification in a conscious, self-chosen way, it is interesting to note that the group identification is clearly exhibited in their clothing and general style choices. In a probably not so ideologically conscious way, but following the need to align themselves to a particular group of people and thus an attitudinal position, the girls in the pictures are taking a clearly subversive and rebellious stance, as their choice for this stylistic identification aligns them with groups and behaviors that are considered deviant by the mainstream and their own community. Many of the girls who show themselves in sexy outfits and who are very probably dressed up for a special situation or event, such as a party, are contesting, among other things, the school rules regarding prudishness and behavior, whereby, as explained by psychologists and scholars Jill Denner and Bianca Guzmán, "the dress code prohibitions at once sexualize adolescent female bodies and discipline that sexuality. Girls who do not conform to the dress code are marked as sexually immoral and destined for teenage pregnancy and academic failure" (101). In a way, these girls manage to defy and challenge these codes but similarly expose themselves in a highly patriarchal discourse where they are seen and valued as objects of male desire.

The observation and analysis of the numerous photographs and images of the Los Angeles *barrio* life and youth experience in the Nineties bring me to the following conclusions: clothes and external outfits are tremendously important for these young girls, as they link them to their peers, their *barrio*, and finally they identify them ethnically too. In general terms, this often reinforces those traits that are considered feminine in patriarchal terms and they consciously turn themselves into objects of desire. Thus, the clothing choices preferred by these young girls are those that are labeled in terms of a masculine, patriarchal gaze and gender hierarchization, where women are the objects of such a gaze and eventually male desire. In this sense, these young *Chola* girls, or girls who adopt a markedly *Chola* look, present an attitude of *deviation and subversion through the conscious* by means of adopting the look that identifies them with the *Cholo* world, and thus an underground subculture. On the other hand, this move also positions them in a situation of unconscious acceptance of the very constraining gender roles that have kept women tied to the norms of beauty and physical appearance mandated by the mainstream, patriarchal (sexual) norm.

The second conclusion that I reach by examining the abundant array of photographs shared by their own protagonists and collected and arranged in the various social media are an attempt to make visible a collective that had been (and still is) overlooked, invisibilized and often even criminalized by the mainstream normative look, is that attitude, pose and body language are as relevant as clothing *per se* for these young girls. There other kind of photographs that exemplify said relevance of the pose and attitude, which becomes a whole system of communication for these girls, together with their purely physical look (clothes, makeup and hairstyle).

Many of the girls in said photographs of the Nineties are exemplary of the adherence and communal performance of a group-identifying look. In many cases, and regardless of their individual life choices, they present a look that can be described as a *Chola* "tomboy style" (Vigil). In most of the photographs, the girls are wearing baggy, masculine pants, Pendleton shirts, long dark hair and exaggerated makeup (lipstick and very marked eyeliner), which reinforce their feminine facial traits (eyes, lips, and hair). The reproduction of this look is adapted in varying degrees (with different styles of clothing and/or hairstyle or makeup), but they all conform to a homogeneous, unifying image that describes them as a united group of girls, linked by their life situations probably, and in this particular case by a very definite group look. What is interesting in these photographs is that the girls who pose in diverse group-gang poses seek no position as objects of desire, and their look is totally devoid of any sexualized trait. Their baggy pants and big shirts or t-shirts leave no room for bodily exposure, and their femininity (once again, considered in patriarchal terms) stems from their makeup and hairstyle. However, what in my view needs to be highlighted is their pose and attitude as individuals and as a group. Undoubtedly, these group representations are elaborated ones, in the sense that the girls are posing for the picture. In many of the cases, the girls have grave looks and faces, and their heads and eyes look slightly upwards, communicating and presenting a feeling of pride, roughness, strength, and finally defiance. They choose to be represented as a group, and as a group they also present a conscious stance of subversion and rebellion, and, in sum, aggressiveness. In many cases, their defiant, almost belligerent look conveys the idea that these groups are to be respected and even feared. Once more, their group image, demonstrated by their homogeneous clothing and, moreover, their serious and strong poses and attitude, gives these girls a position of conscious subversive and rebellious women, whose communal image may well connect them to the stereotypical gang look. Consequently, their body language transmits the idea that they have to be respected and finally taken into account. Their subversion, which is performed consciously, is addressed not only to the mainstream society but also their own community, which they consciously deviate from with the above-described performance of assertiveness. As with other subcultural groups, their "clothes express the attitude of the wearer and therefore mirror the aesthetic, moral and nationalistic ideals of those who wear them" (Cunningham and Voso Lab, 6). In this case, moreover, they express their attitude towards their ethnic, class and gender social expectations, which thus marks them as deviant. As a consequence, as affirmed by Abelardo Valdez, "once involved in the gang, girls are stigmatized by traditional Mexican American gender norms that label them as a 'bad girl'" (5).

The visual identification of the girls with a group (which is probably a gang) can be seen in many of the photographs also through the performance of the hand sign language that characterizes gangs. In some of them, the girls not only show this sense of belonging and being part of something structured such as a gang through the homogeneity of their clothing and general style, but also because they are conveying a clear, direct message through their group's sign language. In many of the cases, the girls are writing the name and symbology of their group with their hands, and are thus connecting themselves to a particular group and therefore to a particular position towards the general social norms and regulations.

Similarly, I consider it relevant to highlight the fact that in many of the visual representations of young girls of the Nineties, they are posing next to/with a car, the ultimate symbol of (juvenile) freedom, but also of masculinity. Cars as symbols of freedom, speed, choice, power and control have, from their first appearance, related to men. It was not until the, second half of the 20th century, long after cars became a common good for families, that women could drive. In the case of the *Latino/Chicano* community in the United States, the car, and especially the concept of low riding as a means of public exposure and vindication of a place in society, has always been linked to men, and thus connected to masculinity. In sociologist Charles Tatum's words, low riding or even owning a car was "distinctly male dominated and mirrored the rigidly hierarchical and patriarchal roles of women and men in the wider context of *Chicana/o* culture in general and more particularly in the working-class segment of the *Chicana/o* population" (139). These girls' attitude, posing next to a car and sometimes standing on it, turns it into an ornamental element of the picture, where the girls are protagonists but so too is the car. The fact that these girls adhere physically and visually to an identifiable *Chola* style, that they link themselves to a gang by means of their hand gestures and finally that they supposedly own a car describes them as free, independent women. In addition to this, in much of the literature and in many of the cinematographic depictions of gang life, a car is recurrently presented as essential for 'doing business.' A car not only helps gang members to carry out their generally illegal business, but is often used as a system of surveillance of both their own turf and that of others. Drive-by shootings are recurrent in many of the real and fictional accounts of gang activity. The women in some of the photographs own a car and are thus identified as nondependent women. The car, in sum, becomes part of the extralinguistic language that the girls in the photograph utilize to define themselves as consciously subversive, voiced, independent women.

To conclude this revision of the meaning of the language that *Cholas* in the Nineties adopted and followed as a symbol of their group and ethnic identification, the following remark needs to be made: the fact that a young woman shares and dresses in the *Chola* style does not necessarily imply that she belongs to a particular gang, and thus to any kind of illegal activity. However, it is also true that, as seen in most of the photographs I observed, this particular style is powerful in terms of the message it conveys. For some of the girls, it just represents a link to their peers and, moreover, a sexy way to show themselves to the men of their group. Vigil explains that

> [i]n the gang subculture, many other symbolic features – movements, sounds, and images – are used to characterize the street and cultural identity of gang members. The dress, walk, talk, and body language are distinct and assert a streetwise sense of control and command of life's challenges and threats. Particularly fascinating in this regard is the dress and style of female gang members. For example, exaggerated makeup, tattoos, and hairstyle can send messages to onlookers and provide means to show power or a way to mask the former identity of the person who is now a gang member. Some females adopt the dress style of khakis and gang garb, but those who wish to flaunt their sexuality or indicate that they accept being a sex object dress in very skimpy clothing. The same girl may alternate between these dress styles, depending on the occasion.
>
> (*Rainbow* 48–9)

In any case, as indicated in the previous analysis and in the above words, their style connects them, at least symbolically, to a certain gang structure, and thus defines them as *consciously subversive and deviant* women. On the one hand, this is because their look defies the norms related to female decency and proper attitude. Most of the girls who have been observed present aggressive, defiant attitudes, manners and postures, which could be interpreted as an aggressive and defiant attitude to society as a whole. On the other hand, their look connects them to a life system and a set of beliefs, that of the gang life, which directly confronts the mainstream laws and social codes of behavior. However, bearing in mind the wide array of proof that shows that these young girls and women live in a situation of educational, economic and social marginalization, their defiance is targeted mostly at the system that keeps them in said harsh situation. In particular, the girls and boys who are seeking a way out within the gang system are consciously escaping and looking for shelter and recognition within the gang, which represents a social structure that accounts for their existence and takes care of them. With the girls, in most cases they join it in an almost inevitable way, and finally end up unconsciously subverting the norms through a conscious subversion against the norms of dress, style and, in sum, behavior. However, and as the photographs prove, many of these women are represented as women with a voice, who show themselves as empowered women, and who deploy said voice and power throughout their body language, particularly *Chola* style, which presents what Valdez calls *paradoxical autonomy*, in the sense that

> [t]hese contemporary "deviant" females involved in antisocial behaviors seem to be exhibiting a greater variation of autonomy than their counterparts in the past. This autonomy is noncelebratory. (. . .) Collectively, these women continue to live in an ethnic community that continues to impose clearly

defined gender and class barriers on women. Thus, their relative autonomy from men has not necessarily resulted in a freer development of self, as celebratory autonomy would assume.

(7)

Following Valdez's line of thought, I would define their subversion and rebellion as an *ambivalent subversion and deviation through the conscious*, as they reject an array of social norms of conduct with their clothes and behavior, and in a parallel way they often accept the hierarchical gender roles of their community and, in particular, of their gang or group. This is done either by showing themselves as objects of male desire or, on the contrary, by reproducing male ways in terms of style, look, body language, and social attitude and behavior.

Chapter 7

Concluding remarks

Clothes, clothing, fashion, and individual style are, in the Western world, essential markers of a person's (and a group's) social identification. Given that the first and probably most essential function of clothing is that of protecting the body from external influences (such as climate), this project has stemmed from the premise that the cultural signification of clothing and clothing choices is evident. Clothes cover the naked body and therefore turn the human body into a social, socialized and thus cultured entity. Similarly, clothes communicate and express characteristics of the individual wearing them that connect her/him to a particular historical moment, a certain social class, a given gender, a concrete task and, as we have seen in these pages, to a given ideology.

The communicative function of clothing, therefore, is undeniable. In the case of the young communities of any Western country or community, and particularly after the 20th and 21st centuries, where the young have become a 'group of their own,' subject to the influences of consumption, the clothing choices that they make connect them to, or disconnect them from, a particular group of young people. This group identification and affiliation may occur around a given musical fashion, or, as in the case of the three groups that we have focused upon in these pages, a given attitude (and thus ideology) to the particular sociohistorical moment that their protagonists live. In the case of young groups that are considered subcultural (and thus marginal and/or alternative) to the mainstream line of thought, dress and moral/social conduct, dress and clothing choices are used as a means of group expression and ideological identification. Said identification and subversive, confrontational attitude towards 'the norm' may be a conscious choice, such as in the case of the punk movement in Great Britain, but in other cases it is driven by less articulated ideological and political positions and agendas, regardless of the fact that their subversive effect may be interpreted as a direct affront to the status quo as well.

In the case of women, the strict moral, physical and behavioral codes that they have been subjected to have marked their identity as social and individual beings throughout the ages. The first accounts of human decency (and indecency) found in the Bible, for example, mark women as conveyors of sin, and thus strong control of their morality and rights has been implemented through several historical periods and generations. Thus, the dressing and attitudinal codes of women have always been clearly and strictly defined, and any deviance from the norm by 'different' women has always been regarded as a complete and violent attack on the social well-being of the whole community. These women, ostracized and considered in negative light, regarded as loose and whore-like, have therefore repeatedly been betrayers of the communal cause.

The case of women of Mexican American origin in the United States, as well as that of other female groups that are not part of the dominant cultural and political group, is of particular interest, as the moral and behavioral pressure exerted upon them arises from diverse and convergent sources. These women, as part (a discriminated against part) of North American society, have endured all the moral codes that US women have known. In addition, their very patriarchal and gender hierarchical Mexican tradition, which in a way is aimed at protecting them from the external aggressions of the more permissive US Anglo social life in the name of the group's cultural tradition and heritage, has left them in a situation of social isolation and control by the group. Moreover, the obvious class and ethnic discrimination and second-class status of their own group have left these women in a situation of oblivion and transparency, as well as with fewer educational sources than other women in the country with better sociocultural options.

However, as has occurred historically in all communities and sociohistorical traditions, there are always deviant voices that seek to change their personal and group situations. This is the case with the female communities that have been the focus of this work. Their lives and destinies clearly marked for them, these women chose to defy the rules and create a life of their own – some of them through their physical presence on the streets, others with their voices and elaborate political ideologies as well. In any case, the three groups of women who have been observed in these pages are (r)evolutionary women, women with a voice, who have fought to adapt and improve their situation, as well as that of their peers and their community.

The case of *Pachucas* was a direct affront to the puritanistic, patriotic US society of the Forties and their own too-patriarchal and patronizing community's tradition. By dressing differently, showing their knees, wearing big pants and male suits, but mostly by being and becoming visible on the street, the *Pachucas* started a revolution and were defiant, brave and spoke for themselves in front of a society that had chosen not to see them. Criminalized and insulted, labeled as prostitutes and dangerous women, the *Pachucas'* 'only' achievement was to defy not only their personal situation but also the subjugated, colonized reality of their own people. However, for both them and their male counterparts, "the 'way out' zoot suit look stretched dominant constructions of masculinity and femininity until they were called into question" (Macías 107). The photographs we can observe from that time, (which are undoubtedly not enough to draw any scientifically proved conclusions, but just perceptions and feelings) are proof that *Pachucas* enjoyed the chance that World War II was giving them to 'live the streets' and choose their own destiny. *Pachucas* were, therefore, unconscious revolutionaries, whose life attitude and bodily experience turned them into political beings, whose bodies and social attitude became a strong ideological tool – feminine and political, feminist and revolutionary.

The case of *Chicanas*, in contrast, presents a group of women whose political engagement was highly elaborated and their demands consciously articulated. Theirs was a double struggle: on the one hand, *Chicanas* joined the general *Causa* demands for social justice and equality for people of non-Anglo origin, and in particular for people of Mexican descent; on the other, *Chicanas* mostly demanded full control of their lives, bodies, sexualities, educational and social choices in a society that still did not want to see them, and a community that was too patriarchal and chauvinistic. The *Chicanas'* attitude towards life and society was, therefore, political, as was their message. It is, at this point, interesting to note that, in the case of this group, which aligned itself in terms of style and mood with the prevalent hippie-like atmosphere that existed among the United States youth in the Sixties and Seventies, their look was natural and not clearly marked in terms of gender identification. The *Chicanas'* natural, casual look rejected any kind of ornamentation that would make reference to, or comply with, the aesthetic gender norms that women (and men) have forever been subjected to. Thus, natural hairstyles, clean faces devoid of any makeup and comfortable clothes that did not necessarily convey a gender mark were the general rule for the *Chicana* activists of the Sixties and Seventies. Bodies were thus not understood and conceived as means of ideological subversion and demand, but were ideological, subversive and political *per se*. The individual choice to make about the body was political *per se*. The *Chicanas*, therefore, were conscious revolutionaries and their bodies, lives and political engagement subversive in essence.

Cholas, for their part, and their ideological, subversive use and exposure of their bodies and physical appearance are, in my view, ambivalent and clearly respond to what Vigil has defined as a situation of "multiple marginality." As we have seen in the previous pages, the Nineties were a time of economic prosperity in the United States, the civil rights and feminist movements had paved the way for the opening of (some more) choices and breaking of (some) borders that had kept women and people of color in difficult situations. In this apparently positive situation, however, life in many US *barrios* and ghettos was not as easy and positive as outside its borders, and the achievements of the Sixties were not as obvious and evident. In this context, the situation of many young *barrio* people could be considered marginal and deprived, and gangs and gang activity turned into an economic, social, and personal way out for many young men and women of these deprived *barrios*.

These alternative structures to the normative society were arranged in a highly hierarchical way, as well as within very strict patriarchal and gender parameters. Gangs are mostly male organizations and the role of women in them is generally more passive. Women in them or who are influenced by them are, in general terms, companions or auxiliaries to the male gang activity. In this context, the situation of many young girls in the Nineties US barrios was, to say the very least, difficult and complicated. Visual accounts of these women show that they adopt two tendencies in terms of style and social identification: Some adopt a "feminine" style and others a more "masculine" one, as expressed by Vigil (155). The former fully comply 'ready for the boys,' adopting a highly sexualized attitude and image. They present themselves as objects of sexual desire, and in this sense use their bodies and physicality to attract boys and thus become part of their community. In contrast, the girls who choose to adopt a more assertive physical look, and reproduce a feminine version of the masculine gang style are, to me, strong women who, with their look and attitude, express agency, control over their lives and, moreover, a challenging, proud and thus empowered, rebellious attitude to a society that is oblivious to and rejects them. The representations of these women show some similarities to those of *Pachucas*, regardless of the obvious differences that exist between the two groups in terms of the social, cultural and, in sum, historical periods that they both lived in. Both *Pachucas* and *Cholas* in the Nineties chose to adapt the male attire to their own, feminizing the male zoot suit or even masculinizing their feminine attire. In this sense, both the *Pachucas* and the *Cholas* explicitly break the male/female gender division that clothing so clearly marks. A male attire worn and redescribed by a self-conscious woman becomes a female attire conveying a clear political and ideological message: gender barriers are no longer accepted and embodied by these women. On the other hand, the sometimes 'exaggerated' feminization that both *Pachucas* and *Cholas* demonstrated through their makeup and hairstyles once again depicts a high degree of agency and personal will on the part of these women, who chose to reinterpret the beauty myth (Wolf) intricately designed and conceived for women and make it their own in a self-conscious way. In sum, both *Pachucas* and *Cholas*, who could be considered less politically conscious than *Chicana* activists, conduct a clear conscious revolution through their physical appearance, and thus become (unconsciously) highly political beings, whose bodies transmit rebellion, subversion and a defense of difference. *Pachucas*, *Chicanas* and *Cholas*: three generations of women who have dressed to exist, dressed to resist.

Bibliography

"The 1960s History." www.history.com/topics/1960s/1960s-history. Web. October 18, 2018.
Acuña, Rodolfo. *Occupied America: A History of Chicanos*, 5th ed. New York, San Francisco: Pearson, Longman, 2002 (1981).
Alaniz, Yolanda and Megan Cornish. *Viva La Raza: A History of Chicano Identity & Resistance*. Seattle: Red Letter Press, 2008.
Anzaldúa, Gloria. *Borderlands. La Frontera. The New Mestiza*. San Francisco, CA: Aunt Lute Books, 1987.
Barnard, Malcolm. *Fashion as Communication*, 2nd ed. London, New York: Routledge, 2002 (1996).
———. *Fashion Theory: A Reader*. London, New York: Routledge, 2006.
———. *Fashion Theory: An Introduction*. London, New York: Routledge, 2014.
Barthes, Roland. *The Fashion System*. Translated By M. Ward and R. Howard. New York: Hill and Wang, 1983 (1967).
Batterberry, Michael and Ariane Ruskin Batterberry. *Mirror, Mirror: A Social History of Fashion*. New York: Holt, Rinehart and Winston, 1977.
Bebout, Lee. *Mythohistorical Interventions: The Chicano Movement and Its Legacies*. Minneapolis, London: U of Minnesota P, 2011.
Blea, Irene I. *La Chicana and the Intersection of Race, Class and Gender*. New York, Westport, CT: Praeger, 1992.
Blumer, Herbert. "Fashion: From Class Differentiation to Collective Selection." *Sociological Quarterly* 10.3 (1969): 275–91.
Boucher, François. *20,000 Years of Fashion: The History of Costume and Personal Adornment*. New York: Harry N. Abrams, Inc. Publishers, 1983 (1965).
Bourdieu, Pierre. *Distinction: A Social Critique of Judgment of Taste*. London: Routledge & Kegan Paul, 1984.
Brake, Mike. *Comparative Youth Culture: The Sociology of Youth Culture and Youth Subcultures in America, Britain and Canada*. London, New York: Routledge, 1990.
Breward, Christopher. *The Culture of Fashion: A New History of Fashionable Dress*. Manchester, New York: Manchester UP, 1995.
Cabral, Diana. *Fashion Aesthetics: The Legacy of Chicana Fashion on Identity Development*. Diss. California State U, Northridge, 2014.
Calefato, Patrizia. *The Clothed Body*. Translated by Lisa Adams. Oxford, New York: Berg, 2004.

Campbell, Anne. *The Girls in the Gang*. New York: Basil Blackwell, 1984.
———. "Female Participation in Gangs." In *Gangs in America*, edited by Ronald C. Huff. Thousand Oaks, CA: Sage Publications, 1990: 163–82.
Campbell, Neil, ed. *The Radiant Hour: Versions of Youth in American Culture*. Exeter: U of Exeter P, 2000.
Carlyle, Thomas. *Sartor Resartus*. Edited by K. McSweeney and P. Sabor. Oxford: Oxford UP, 1987 (1933–34).
Chafe, William H. "The Paradox of Progress." In *Our American Sisters: Women in American Life and Thought*, edited by Jean E. Friedman and William G. Shade. Boston, London: Allyn and Bacon, Inc., 1976: 385–401.
Chávez, Jennie V. "Women of the Mexican American Movement." In *Chicana Feminist Thought: The Basic Historical Writings*, edited by Alma M. García. New York, London: Routledge, 1997: 36–9.
Clarke, John. "Style." In *Resistance Through Rituals: Youth Subcultures in Post-War Britain*, edited by Stuart Hall and Toni Jefferson. London: Routledge, 2006 (1975): 147–61.
Clarke, John, Stuart Hall, Tony Jefferson and Brian Roberts. "Subcultures, Cultures and Class: A Theoretical Overview." In *Resistance Through Rituals: Youth Subcultures in Post-War Britain*, edited by Stuart Hall and Tony Jefferson. London: Routledge, 2006 (1975).
Cohen, Stanley. *Folk Devils and Moral Panics: The Creation of the Mods and the Rockers*. London: Routledge, 2002 (1972).
Correa, Jennifer G. "The Targeting of the East Los Angeles Brown Berets by a Racial Patriarchal Capitalist State: Merging Intersectionality and Social Movement Research." *Critical Sociology* 37.1 (2010): 83–101.
Cotera, Martha. *Diosa y Hembra: The History and Heritage in Chicanas in the U.S.* Austin, TX: Information System Development, 1976.
Crane, Diana. *Fashion and Its Social Agendas: Class, Gender, and Identity in Clothing*. Chicago, London: The U of Chicago P, 2000.
Cunningham, Patricia A. and Susan Voso Lab. *Dress and Popular Culture*. Bowling Green, OH: Popular Press, 1991.
Davis, Fred. *Fashion, Culture and Identity*. Chicago, London: The U of Chicago P, 1992.
De Beauvoir, Simone. *The Second Sex*. New York: Vintage Books, 2010 (1949).
De Clerq, Eva. *The Seduction of the Female Body: Women's Rights in Need of a New Body Politics*. Basingstoke: Palgrave Macmillan, 2013.
Del Castillo, Adelaida R. "La Visión Chicana." In *Chicana Feminist Thought: The Basic Historical Writings*, edited by Alma M. García. New York, London: Routledge, 1997: 44–8.
Denner, Jill and Bianca L. Guzmán. *Latina Girls: Voices of Adolescent Strength in the United States*. New York: New York UP, 2006.
Descartes, René. *A Discourse on Method*. London: Dent, 1924 (1637).
Dietrich, Lisa C. *Chicana Adolescents. Bitches, Ho's, and Schoolgirls*. Westport, CT, London: Praeger, 1998.
Eco, Umberto. "Social Life as Sign System." In *Structuralism: An Introduction*, edited by D. Robey. Oxford: Oxford UP, 1972.
Entwistle, Joan. *The Fashioned Body: Fashion, Dress and the Modern Social Theory*. Cambridge: Polity Press, 2000.
Entwistle, Joan and Elizabeth Wilson, "The Body Clothed." In *Catalogue 100 Years of Art and Fashion*. London: Hayward Gallery, 1998.

———. *Body Dressing*. Oxford, New York: Berg, 2001.

Escobedo, Elizabeth R. *From Coveralls to Zoot Suits: The Lives of Mexican American Women on the World War II Home Front*. Chapel Hill: The U of North Carolina P, 2013.

Espinoza, Dionne. "Revolutionary Sisters: Women Solidarity and Collective Identification among Chicana Brown Berets in East Los Angeles: 1967–1970." *Aztlan* 26.1 (Spring 2001): 17–58.

Fields, Rona Marcia. *The Brown Berets: A Participant Observation Study of Social Action in the Schools of Los Angeles*. Dissertation. U of Southern California, Los Angeles. January 1970.

Flores Niemann, Yolanda, S. H. Armitage, et al. eds. *Chicana Leadership*. Lincoln, London: U of Nebraska P, 2002.

Flügel, John Carl. *The Psychology of Clothes*. London: The Hogarth Press and the Institute of Psychoanalysis, 1930.

Friedan, Betty. *The Feminine Mystique*. New York: W. W. Norton & Company, Inc., 1963.

García, Alma M., ed. *Chicana Feminist Thought: The Basic Historical Writings*. New York, London: Routledge, 1997.

García, Mario T. *The Chicano Generation: Testimonios of the Movement*. Berkeley: U of California P, 2015.

Gelder, Ken. *Subcultures: Cultural Histories and Social Practice*. London, New York: Routledge, 2007.

Genesis 2:25. *The Bible*. Standard English Version.

———. 3: 6–7. *The Bible*. Standard English Version.

———. 3: 10–11. *The Bible*. Standard English Version.

Goffman, Erving. *Stigma: Notes on the Management of a Spoiled Identity*. New York: Simon & Schuster, 1963.

Goode, Erich and Nachman Ben-Yahuda. *Moral Panics: Social Construction of Deviance*. Malden, MA: Blackwell Publishers, 1994.

Goodson, Aileen. "Nudity in Ancient to Modern Cultures." www.primitivism.com/nudity.htm.

Gordon, Milton M. "The Concept of the Sub-Culture and its Application." *Social Forces* 26.1 (1947): 40–2.

Grady, John. "The Scope of Visual Sociology." *Visual Studies* 11.2 (January 1996): 10–24.

Gramsci, Antonio. *Selection from the Prison Notebooks of Antonio Gramsci*. Edited and translated by Geoffrey Smith and Quintin Hoare. New York: International Publishers Co., 1971.

Griffin, Christine. *Representations of Youth: The Study of Youth and Adolescence in Britain and America*. Cambridge: Polity Press, 1993.

Guy, Ali, Eileen Green and Maura Banim. *Through the Wardrobe. Women's Relationships with Their Clothes*. Oxford, New York: Berg, 2003.

Haenfler, Ross. *Subcultures: The Basics*. London, New York: Routledge, 2014.

Hall, Stuart and Tony Jefferson, eds. *Resistance Through Rituals: Youth Subcultures in Post-War Britain*. London: Routledge, 2006 (1975).

Hebdige, Dick. *Subculture: The Meaning of Style*. London: Methuen, 1979.

Horn, Marilyn J. *The Second Skin: An Interdisciplinary Study of Clothing*. Reno: U of Nevada P, 1968.

Kaiser, Susan. "Minding Appearances: Style, Truth, and Subjectivity." In *Body Dressing*, edited by Joanne Entwistle and Elizabeth Wilson. Oxford, New York: Berg, 2001: 79–102.

Kiger, Patrick J. "The '90s: The Last Great Decade?" *National Geographic*. http://channel.nationalgeographic.com/the-90s-the-last-great-decade/.
Levi-Strauss, C. *The Savage Mind*. London: Weidenfeld and Nicolson, 1966.
———. *Totemism*. London: Penguin, 1969.
Longueaux y Vasquez, Enriqueta. "The Mexican American Woman." *Sisterhood Is Powerful: An Anthology of Writings from the Women's Liberation Movement*, edited by Robin Morgan. New York: Vintage Books, 1970.
Lurie, Alison. *The Language of Clothes*. London: Bloomsbury, 1992.
Lynch, Annette. *Dress, Gender and Cultural Change: Asian American and African American Rites of Passage*. Oxford, New York: Berg, 1999.
Macías, Anthony. *Mexican American Mojo: Popular Music, Dance, and Urban Culture in Los Angeles, 1935–1963*. Durham, London: Duke UP, 2008.
Maffesoli, Michel. *The Time of the Tribes: The Decline of Individualism in Mass Society*. London: Sage, 1996.
McEuen, Melissa A. *Making War, Making Women. Femininity and Duty on the American Homefront, 1941–1945*. Athens, Georgia: U of Georgia P, 2011.
McRobbie, Angela. *Feminism and Youth Culture: From Jackie to Just Seventeen*. Houndmills: Palgrave Macmillan, 1997.
McRobbie, Angela and Jenny Garber. "Girls and Subcultures: an Exploration." In *Resistance Through Rituals: Youth Subcultures in Post-War Britain*, edited by Stuart Hall and Tony Jefferson. London: Routledge, 2006 (1975): 177–88.
Mendoza-Denton, N. "Muy Macha: Gender and Ideology in Gang Girls' Discourse About Makeup." *Ethos* 61 (1996): 47–63.
Merleau-Ponty, M. *The Primacy of Perception*. Evanston, IL: Northwestern UP, 1976.
Miller, Jody. "The Girls in the Gang: What We've Learned from Two Decades of Research." In *Gangs in America III*, edited by Ronald C. Huff. Thousand Oaks, London: Sage Publications, 2002: 175–98.
Miranda, Marie. "Keta." In *Homegirls in the Public Sphere*. Austin, TX: U of Texas P, 2003.
Moore, Joan W. *Going Down to the Barrio: Homeboys and Homegirls in Change*. Philadelphia: Temple UP, 1991.
Muñoz, Carlos Jr. *Youth, Identity, Power: The Chicano Movement*. Revised and expanded ed. London, New York: Verso, 2007 (1989).
Muñoz, José Esteban. *Disidentifications: Queers of Color and the Performance of Politics*. Minneapolis, London: U of Minnesota P, 1999.
———. "Prehistoric Clothing." In *Encyclopedia of Fashion*. www.fashionencyclopedia.com/fashion_costume_culture/The-Ancient-WorldPrehistoric/Prehistoric-Clothing.html. Web. February 25, 2016.
"The National Organization for Women's 1966 Statement of Purpose." https://now.org/about/history/statement-of-purpose/.
Nieto-Gómez, Anna. "La Chicana: Legacy of Suffering and Self-Denial." In *Chicana Feminist Thought: The Basic Historical Writings*, edited by Alma M. García. New York, London: Routledge, 1997a: 48–50.
———. "Sexism in the Movimiento." In *Chicana Feminist Thought: The Basic Historical Writings*, edited by Alma M. García. New York, London: Routledge, 1997b: 97–100.
Obregón Pagán, Eduardo. *Murder at the Sleepy Lagoon: Zoot Suits, Race & Riot in Wartime L.A.* Chapel Hill, London: U of North Carolina P, 2003.

Orozco, Cynthia E. "Sexism in Chicano Studies and the Community." In *Chicana Voices: Intersection of Class, Race and Gender*. Austin, TX: Center for Mexican American Studies, U of Texas P, 1990.

———. *No Mexicans, Women or Dogs Allowed: The Rise of the Mexican American Civil Rights Movement*. Austin, TX: U of Texas P, 2009.

Orozco, Enrique. C. *The Chicano Labyrinth of Solitude: A Study in the Making of the Chicano Mind and Character*. Dubuque, IA: Kendall/Hunt Publishing Company, 1996.

Parkins, Wendy, ed. *Fashioning the Body Politic: Dress, Gender, Citizenship*. Oxford, New York: Berg, 2002.

Phillips, Susan A. *Wallbangin'. Graffiti and Gangs in L.A.* Chicago, IL: U of Chicago P, 1999.

Portillos, Edwardo Luis. "Women, Men, and Gangs: The Social Construction of Gender in the Barrio." In *Female Gangs in America*, edited by Meda Chesney-Lind and John Haggerdon. Chicago, IL: U of Illinois P, 1999.

Ramírez, Catherine S. *The Woman in the Zoot Suit: Gender, Nationalism, and the Cultural Politics of Memory*. Durham, London: Duke UP, 2009.

Roach, Marie Ellen and Joanne B. Eicher. "The Language of Personal Adornment." In *The Fabrics of Culture*, edited by Justine Cordwell & Ronad Schwarz, et al. The Hague: Mouton, 1979, 7–22.

Rorabaugh, W. J. *American Hippies*. Cambridge: U of Washington P, 2015.

Rouse, Elizabeth. *Understanding Fashion*. Oxford: BSP Professional Books, 1989.

Rubinstein, Ruth P. *Dress Codes: Meanings and Messages in American Culture*, 2nd ed. Boulder, CO: Westview Press, 2001.

Rudofsky, Bernard. *Are Clothes Modern? An Essay on Contemporary Apparel*. P. Theobold, 1947.

Ruiz, Vicki L. *From Out of the Shadows: Mexican Women in Twentieth Century America*. Oxford: Oxford UP, 2008 (1998).

Short, James. "New Wine in Old Bottles? Change and Continuity in American Gangs." In *Gangs in America*, edited by Ronald Huff. Thousand Oaks, CA: Sage Publications, 1990: 223–39.

Simmel, Georg. "Fashion." *American Journal of Sociology* 62.6 May 1957 (1904): 541–8.

Soper, Kate. "Dress Needs: Reflections on the Clothed Body, Selfhood and Consumption." In *Body Dressing*, edited by Joanne Entwistle and Elizabeth Wilson. Oxford, New York: Berg, 2001: 13–32.

"Style." www.merriam-webster.com/dictionary/style.

Sweetman, Paul. "Shop-Window Dummies? Fashion, the Body, and Emergent Socialities." *Body Dressing*, edited by Joanne Entwistle and Elizabeth Wilson, Oxford, New York, 2001: 59–77.

Tatum, Charles M. *Lowriders in Chicano Culture: From Low to Slow to Show*. Santa Barbara: Greenwood Press, 2011.

Taylor, Lou. *The Study of Dress History*. Manchester, New York: Manchester UP, 2002.

Ulrich, John M. and Andrea Harris, eds. *GenXegesis: Essays on Alternative Youth (sub) Culture*. Madison: The U of Wisconsin P, 2003.

Valdez, Abelardo. *Mexican American Girls and Gang Violence: Beyond Risk*. New York: Palgrave Macmillan, 2007.

Valdivia, Angharad N. and Rhiannon S. Bettivia. "Girl Culture: We Must Continue to Revisit It." *A Latina in the Land of Hollywood and Other Essays on Media Culture*, edited by Angharad N. Valdivia. Tucson: The U of Arizona P, 2000: 23–41.

Veblen, Thorstein. *The Theory of the Leisure Class: An Economic Study of Institutions.* London: Unwin Books, 1970 (1899).

Vigil, James Diego. *Barrio Gangs. Street Life and Identity in Southern California.* Austinn: U of Texas P, 1988.

———. *A Rainbow of Gangs. Street Cultures in the Mega-City.* Austin, TX: U of Texas P, 2002.

———. *The Projects: Gang and Non-Gang Families in East Los Angeles.* Austin, TX: U of Texas P, 2007.

———. "Female Gang Members from East Los Angeles." *International Journal of Social Inquiry* 1 (2008): 47–74.

Walford, Jonathan. *Sixties Fashion: From Less Is More to Youthquake.* London: Thames & Hudson, 2013.

Ware, Susan. *American Women's History: A Very Short Introduction.* Oxford: Oxford UP, 2015.

"What Is the Chicana Movement?" *Exploring the Chicana Feminist Movement.* http://umich.edu/~ac213/student_projects07/latfem/latfem/whatisit.html.

Wilson, Elizabeth. *Adorned in Dreams: Fashion and Modernity.* New Brunswick: Rutgers UP, 2003 (1985).

Wolf, Naomi. *The Beauty Myth: How Images of Women Are Used Against Women.* New York: Harper Collins, 2002.

Woloch, Nancy. *Women and the American Experience: A Concise History.* New York, St Louis: Overture Books, 1996.

Woolf, Virginia. *Three Guineas.* London: World's Classics, 1992 (1938).

Williams, Patrick J. *Subcultural Theory: Traditions and Concepts.* Cambridge: Polity Press, 2011.

Index

Note: Page numbers in italics indicate references to figures.

act of dressing *see* getting dressed
Adelitas de Aztlan, Las 68
advertisement function of clothes 11
Anglo liberation movement 64
Anzaldúa, Gloria 79
Arellanes, Gloria 72
Ayes, Edward Durán 41
Aztec eagle 80

Baca, Dora 40
Barnard, Malcolm 12
barrio girls 5 *see also* Cholas
barrios: ecological environment of 92; gang systems and 91; street socialization process 93
Batterberry, Michael and Ariane 21
beauty myth 90
Bible: clothing portrayed as punishment 1–2; on nakedness 8; women as conveyors of sin 105–6
Blea, Irene 76
body: bond between dress and 11; dress linking social being to 15; as site of protest 81, 83
Boucher, François 9
Brake, Mike 30–1
bricolage 31
brown beret, as symbol of pride and unity 68
Brown Berets: adopting indigenous symbols 70; constitutional manifesto 67–8; control over women 72; fighting for social equality 68; formation of 67; homogeneous identity of 74; marriages 69; membership to 67; paramilitary essence of 71–2; segregation of women 68; uniform of 67–8; *see also* Brown Beret women

Brown Beret women: adopting Brown Berets uniformization 68; adopting skirt within uniform 72–3; attire and demeanor of 68–72; experiencing sexism 68; indigenization of 70; organization style abandonment 72–3; photograph of *71*; strict regulations for 69; style and behavior of 68; *see also* Brown Berets

Cabral, Diana 79
Calefato, Patrizia 14
Caló 4
Campbell, Anne 96
Carlyle, Thomas 10
cars: low riding 102; as symbols of freedom 102
Catholic Church 63–5
Center for Contemporary Cultural Studies (CCCS) 26
Chanel 59
chaperonage 35
Chávez, César 62, 80, *80*
Chávez, Helen 58
Chicana feminist movement 18, 54, 57–8, 65–6, 70, 86
Chicana feminists: clashing with *Movimiento* 64; clash with white feminists 58; cultural nationalism and 63–4; definition of 4; demand for civil rights 74; joining *Movimiento Chicano* 58
Chicanas: adopting hippie symbols 84–6; body as conveyer of political message 81; body language 78; colonization of 65; as conscious political activists 28, 107; defending sociocultural/ethnic belonging 28–9; demonstrating deviant

position 32; deviant and contestational attitude of 76–9; differential identification of 31; discrimination against 64–5; double articulation of 29; educational opportunities 90; empowerment of 59; gender role rebellion of 18; hippie-like atmosphere of 107; hyperfeminization of 83; photograph of 77; reclaiming indigenous ancestry 79; subversive style 78–9; *see also* Brown Beret women
Chicana style: Brown Berets 67–74; *Virgen de Guadalupe* 66
chicanismo, definition of 62
Chicano Moratorium Committee antiwar demonstrators *82*
Chicano movement *see Movimiento Chicano*
Chicanos, definition of 4
Cholas: in/around gang system 93–6; attitude at schools 96; characteristics of 29–30; definition of 4; exaggerated feminization 108; gang systems and 29; multiple marginality of 92–4, 107; as objects of sexual desire 108; political discourse of 18; posing next to cars 102; *see also* Chola style
Chola style: as connection to gang structure 103; exaggerated makeup 97–8; eyeliner 97–8; grunge style vs. 89; hand sign language 102; hyperfeminine 99–100; as masculine 97–8; paradoxical autonomy 103–4; as sense of belonging 99; sexual-object role 97; tomboy attitude 97; unifying image of 101
choloization 92–3
Christian Dior 21
Civil Rights Act of 1964 57
Clarke, John 29, 31
class *see* social class/status
clothing/dress: act of 1–2; advertisement function of 11; communicative function of 5, 10, 81, 83–4, 105; as a consumer good 13; cultural side of 10, 12; democratization of 9, 13, 22; function of 2, 8, 9–12; gender differences 11; as group body language 98; as language system 10–1; mass production of 9; as means of communication 81, 83–4; as means of individualistic expression 12; portrayed as punishment 1–2; protective function of 10; Renaissance 9; social indicators in 2; as status marker 12–4; *see also* fashion, getting dressed, style
Cog-Magnons 8
communication, clothing and body expression as act of 5, 10, 81, 83–4, 105
consumerism 3, 26–7, 90
cosmetic industry 39
Coupland, Douglas 88
Crane, Diana 12, 16
cultural functions of clothing 10, 12

Davis, Fred 11, 12
decency 1, 10
Del Castillo, Adelaida R. 64
democratization of clothing 9, 13, 22
denim pants 22
Denner, Jill 100
deviance 25–6, 43–6, 52, 74, 91, 106 *see also* subcultural groups
deviant style 17, 31–2
Díaz, José 40
Dietrich, Lisa C. 97
differential identification 31
Dioran look 21
domestic ideology 55
domestic sphere of women 55, 56, 75
dress *see* clothing/dress, getting dressed
dress codes: challenging 100; for Mexican American women 3; strict 2; women required to follow 2

Eco, Umberto 11
Eisenhower jacket 20–1
empathetic form of sociality 14
Entwistle, Joanne 9, 11, 18
Equal Pay Act of 1963 56
Escobedo, Elizabeth R. 36, 47
Espinoza, Dionne 68, 69–70, 73
ethical positions 1
eyeliner, as 'war paint' 97–8

fashion: as class indicator 13; as cultural trend 15; customers' classification types 15; definition of 2–3, 12–3; exposing individual's bodies 59–60; *haute couture* 13, 21, 59; hippie style 22–3; as mass concept 20; miniskirts 59, 73; Nineties fashion 89–91; ponchos 81, 85–6; responding to social/political changes 17–8; Seventies fashion 23; Sixties fashion 22–3, 59–60; vintage clothing 59–60; during World War II years 20–1; *see also* clothing/dress, style

fashion business 20
female agency 3–4, 18, 61, 70, 72, 78
female gang activity 93–5
female identity *see* personal identity
female rebellion 55–6
feminist movement 18, 55, 59–60, 66, 85, 107
Fields, Rona 68–9
Flügel, John Carl 10
Forties fashion 37–9
French fashion industry 20
Friedan, Betty 55–6, 57

gangs/gang systems: control of women 91; gender roles in 94–5; girls as sexual objects 95; graffiti and 96; Illicit Opportunity Scenario 91; as *la familia* 93; multiple marginality of 92–4; representing norms 93; resistance theory 91; street socialization 92–3; *see also* female gang activity
Garber, Jenny 31
Garcia, Alma M. 64
Gelder, Ken 25
gender/gender roles: Chicanas fighting 28–9; differences, in function of clothes 11; formation of 15; in gang systems 94–5; personal identity of 1; rebellion of 18; social identity of 1; social sanctions 94–5; wartime situation reinforcing 34
General Limitation Order L-85 38
Generation X 88
getting dressed 1–2, 8–9, 11, 16, 19
globalization 24, 88
Gordon, M.M. 25
graffiti 96
group belongingness 42–3
group identification 2–3, 18, 42, 90, 99–100, 105
grunge style 89–90
Guzmán, Bianca 100

Haenfler, Ross 25
Hall, Stuart 28, 29
haute couture 13, 21, 59
Hedbige, Dick 17
Hermanas en La Lucha 68
hippie style 22–3, 59–60, 84–6
Hispanic teenagers 5
homology 26, 30
Horn, Marilyn 43
Huerta, Dolores 58, 62, 80–1, *80*, 85

Hutton, Lauren 60
hyperfeminization 99–100

Illicit Opportunity Scenario 91
indigenous symbols 70, 79–81, 85–6
Industrial Revolution 9, 15
inter-ethnic relationships 35
internal colonialism 63

Jefferson, Tony 29

Kaiser, Susan 14
Kennedy, J.F. 62
Kiger, Patrick J. 87

leisure industry, emergence of 23
Leyvas, Henry 40
low riding 102
LULAC (League of United Latin American Citizens) 58, 61
Lynch, Annette 14

Maffesoli's 'empathetic form of sociality' 14
Malinche, La: as role model 36, 75–6; as sexualized woman 76
McCardell, Claire 21
McRobbie, Angela 31
MECHA (*Movimiento Estudiantil Chicano de Azlán*) 63
media: creating moral panic 26; efforts to criminalize Pachucos 47; supporting categorization of Pachucos vs. Marines 42–4; *see also* Zoot Suit Riots
men of color 65
mestiza woman 79
Mexican Americans, identification processes of 61
Mexican American women: entering leisure world 35; entering workforce 3–4; isolation and control of 106; liberalization of 35–6; metaphorical bedroom of 27; religious and cultural icons influencing 3; restricting socialization of 35; World War II and 35–7; *see also* women of color
Mexican American youth, criminalization and victimization of 53
Mexican immigrants 61, 92
Miller, Jody 93–4
miniskirts 59, 73
Miranda, Marie "Keta" 98
modesty 10

Moore, Joan W. 91
morality 1, 10
moral panic 26
Movimiento Chicano: Chicana feminists joining 58; Chicanas protagonistic position in demonstrations 83–4; description of 4; lack of feminine form in 83; as male domain 62; male peers sexist way to women's demands 74–5; Mexican immigrants and 60–1; protest actions 81–3, *82*; rise of 60–1; sexist reactions of 74–5; urban mobilization of 62–3; *see also* Brown Berets
MUJER 64
multiple marginalization 92, 93–5, 107

nakedness: moral/immoral boundary of 8–9; as natural 8; original sin and 10; as shameful 8–9; *see also* Zoot Suit Riots
National Centers for Disease Control and Prevention 5
National *Chicano* Youth Conference 64
Neanderthal peoples 8
"New Look, The" 21
New York Dress Industry (NYDI) 38
Nieto-Gómez, Anna 64–5
Nineties: in economic terms 87–8; expectations of women in 87–9; Generation X 88; globalization 88
Nineties fashion 89–91
nonwhite women *see* women of color
NOW (National Organization of Women) 57
nudity *see* nakedness

Office of War Information (OWI) 37
oppositional dress/style 23
original sin 10
Orozco, Cynthia E. 61–2, 74–5
Orozco, Enrique C. 96

Pachucas: as affront to mainstream society 18; betraying community and traditions 36; criminalization of 46; defiant attitude and style of 28; definition of 3–4; demonstrating deviant position 31–2; exaggerated feminization 108; general look of 44–5; as immoral women 53; as menace to society 36; as not Mexican enough 47; as passive political activists 18; photograph of *52*; political meaning of 37; as protagonists of silent revolution 28; as racially marked individuals 45–6; role of 39, 51–2; as society delinquents 36–7; symbolic meaning of 45; as threat to patriarchal norm 52; as too American 47; as unconscious revolutionaries 54, 106–7; wearing zoot suits 37; Zoot Suit Riots and 39–44; *see also* Pachuca style
Pachuca style: breaking aesthetic behavior norms 47; expressing rebellion and disconformity 48–51; hairstyles 48, 53; photograph of *49*; as political style 47–8; public representations of 48–51; as rejection of the norm 53; as step toward agency and freedom 54; wearing a zoot suit *50*
Pachucos: criminal activities of 45; media's efforts to criminalize 47
Pagán, Obregón 40, 41–2
patriarchal norms 52, 54, 62, 74, 90, 100
patriarchal roles 35, 102
patriarchy 17, 35, 64, 68
personal identity: constructing 6; dehumanization and 42; gender and 1; quest for 77; unitary dress depriving 54
Phillips, Susan 96
"pinup girl" 21
political power 12
ponchos 81, 85–6
practical function 15
protective function of clothes 10
punk movement 105

Ramirez, Catherine 39, 44–5, 46
Raza Unida Party, La 63
Raza working class 61
'ready-to-wear' businesses 23
Reich, Charles 22
religion 1, 3, 57, 62, 64–5 *see also Virgen de Guadalupe*
Renaissance clothing 9
resistance theory of gang systems 91
Roberts, Brian 29
Roosevelt, Eleanor 33
Rosie the Riveter 34, 37
Rouse, Elizabeth 10
Ruiz, Vicki L. 35

Sánchez, David 67–8
SDS (Students for a Democratic Society) 57
self-expression 22
Seventies fashion 23
sexism 57–8, 64–5, 68

sexual liberation/revolution 22, 28
Shrimpton, Jean 59
Simmel, Georg 12
Sixties fashion 22–3, 59–60
Sleepy Lagoon Defense Committee (SLDC) 41
SNCC (Student Nonviolent Coordinating Committee) 57
social class/status, ethnicity linked to 28
social deviance *see* deviance
social/economic status 12, 13–4
social identification 105, 108
social isolation 106
social norms 2–3, 12, 16, 19, 85, 102–4
social sanctions 94–5
Soper, Kate 11, 42
street socialization 92–3, 94
style: definition of 13, 16; Eisenhower jacket 20–1; expressing uniqueness in 15–6; grunge 89–90; hippie 22–3, 59–60; as process of managing appearance 14; as self-conscious image and ideology 30; skirts 21; subculture and 16–7, 30, 85–6; uniform-like 20; *see also* Chicana style, clothing/dress, fashion, Pachuca style
subcultural groups: definition of 25; Gelder's definition of 25; meaningful symbolism in 30–1; as product of class divisions 26; as second-class citizenry 27; style and 30
subversive style 16–7, 30, 85–6 *see also* style
synthetic materials 21

Tatum, Charles 102
teen pregnancies 5, 96
Tellez, Frank 44
Tijerina, Reyes 62
Title VII of the Civil Rights Act of 1964 57
trousers, adoption of 20–1
Twiggy 59

UFW (United Farm Workers) 58, 80–1
uniform-like style 20
University of Chicago 26

Valdez, Abelardo 101, 103–4
Verdusco, Luis 44
Vigil, James Diego 92, 94–5, 103
vintage clothing 59–60
Virgen de Guadalupe, as role model 36, 66

wage gap 56
Walford, Jonathan 59
war mask 97–8
War Production Board (WPB) 38, 41
WAVES (Women Appointed for Volunteer Emergency Service) 34
white women, image of 38 *see also* women, women of color
Williams, J. Patrick 30
Wilson, Elizabeth 15, 20, 22–3
Woloch, Nancy 55, 56
women: active role outside domestic sphere 56; as conveyors of sin 105–6; discrimination against 57; domestic ideology 55; domestic sphere of 75; Forties fashion 37–9; fulfillment of their femininity 56; in gangs 5; higher education attendance rates 88; mobility of 34; in the Nineties 87–9; oppression of 64; in the Seventies 55–9; wage gap 56; wearing trousers 20–1; *see also* white women, women in the workforce, women of color
Women Airforce Services Pilots (WASP) 34
women in the workforce: economic freedom for 3; during World War II years 33–4
women of color 38, 51, 60, 65 *see also* Mexican American women, white women, women
Women's Army Corp (WAC) 34
World War II: female fashion during 38–9; garment industry and 38; General Limitation Order L-85 38; Mexican American women and 35–7; Office of War Information 37; Rosie the Riveter 34; War Production Board 38; women's role in 33–4

Young Citizens for Community Action (YCCA) 67
youth culture, consuming capabilities of 59

zoot suit 37, 41–3, *50*, 106
Zoot Suit Riots: anti-patriotic attitude of 39; causes of 40–1; as means of ethnic hierarchization 51; media creating panic in 26; Pachucas and 39–44; Pachucof/a outfit as discrimination in 45